God's Whispers: Your Anchor Through Life's Storms

A Memoir by Christine Nekas-Thoma

Scripture taken from the HOLY BIBLE, NEW INTERNATIONAL VERSION®. NIV®. Copyright © 1973, 1978, 1984 by International Bible Society. Used by permission of Zondervan. All rights reserved worldwide.

Higher Ground Books & Media
P.O. Box 2914
Springfield, OH 45501-2914
www.highergroundbooksandmedia.com
1-937-970-0554

This memoir depicts actual events in the life of the author as truthfully as recollection permits. While all persons within are actual individuals, some names and identifying characteristics have been changed to respect their privacy. Some events have been compressed, and some dialogue has been recreated.

The views expressed in the work are solely those of the author and do not necessarily reflect the views of the publisher, and the publisher hereby disclaims any responsibility for them.

ISBN (Paperback): 978-1-955368-25-4

Printed in the United States of America 2022

God's Whispers: Your Anchor Through Life's Storms

A Memoir by Christine Nekas-Thoma

REVIEWS

If you ever listen for God's voice, this is the book for you. This eloquently written first memoir invites you into an intimate journey with Christine as she loses a dear friend and grandparents, navigates relationships and career, faces infertility and other health issues and considers adoption. Learn with her the importance of trust and faith, and a willingness to take God seriously wherever and whenever the signs appear.
—Nancy Flinchbaugh, *Revelation in the Roots: Emerald Isle* and *Letters from the Earth*

Through *God's Whispers: Your Anchor Through Life's Storms*, Christine Nekas-Thoma shares her personal journey to a closer relationship with God, giving examples of God's whispers of affirmation and direction she's learned to recognize in the process. Through the account of a near-death experience in her teens, examples of comfort during tumultuous times in her life, and wisdom she shares along the way, Christine's riveting story offers readers encouragement to hear God speaking in their own lives.
—Barb Geiger*, Paddle for a Purpose*

You can follow Christine on her website at https://christinenekasthoma.com or her Facebook author page at https://www.facebook.com/christinenekasthoma

DEDICATION

This book is dedicated to my dear husband, Phil, whose faith and belief in me made this book possible. Most of what I have learned about love and about trust in God, I have learned from him.

Prologue: Confirmation that God Speaks

Whether you turn to the right or to the left, your ears will hear a voice behind you saying, 'This is the way; walk in it.'
— *Isaiah 30:21.*

In the fall of 2001, I sat in the congregation of Willow Creek Church deeply moved by the pastor's words. He said that God "speaks" to all of us and shared a story to illustrate his point. One evening, God told him to check his basement. It turned out there was a carbon monoxide issue, and had he waited until morning, he would have died in his sleep. This sermon verified to me that I was not crazy for thinking and feeling that God does speak to people in His own ways. In fact, getting confirmation that God speaks reminded me of the time God spoke to me through nature as I sat grieving over the loss of a loved one while writing at Martha's Vineyard. In my journal, I wrote:

> *As I bask on the white sand, I am warmed by the sun's comforting rays. The cool wind's whistling power sneaks up on me as I hear the ebb and flow of the tide quickly pounding against the shore with perfect precision, balance, and rhythm. I can't help but notice how some of the waves are thrown off course as they are interrupted by some massive awe-inspiring red clay rocks that lie between the ocean and the shore. My mind begins to connect the idea that these rocks represent the building blocks of life. As the waves pound into them, they are thrown off course, but just for a little while. The waves continue to flow over and around the rocks that inevitably block them in the short term.*
> *The waves whisper to breathe in, to breathe out in harmony with their natural tide. In and out. It is that simple. As I breathe in positive energy*

*and happily let go of yesterday's storms, I feel newly
baptized with possibilities. In accepting what is, I let go
of what is not. This simple action allows me to continue
to sail with the current instead of against it. In listening
to the magnetic rhythm of the tide, a new pattern forms
in my mind. As a result, I can't help but submit to the
awesome power of God who has been here before, is
now, and will always be.*

God's whisper through the current reminds me of the familiar
words of Philosopher Heraclitus who once said, "The only thing that
is constant is change." Of course, I often resist change because I do
not always know how to go with the flow. Even now as I write this
book, I get temporarily blocked by boulders in my way. In fact,
when life's chaotic storms rage at me, I often must flow without
paddles or life preservers; I can't control what happens. Riding the
waves can be terrifying but necessary.

Death is the ultimate loss of control. When faced with death,
people often have no choice but to ride the last few waves without
life preservers, looking to God for ultimate comfort in their final
days. Many researchers have written not only about death bed
visions as people are between this world and a heavenly one but also
acknowledge that sometimes divine influence tells the dying person
what to say to the living. When my godmother, Margaret, was dying
of cancer, she told me that God said I would someday be a mother of
a little boy. On her death bed, my grandma's words to "keep
writing" seemed prophetic because I have always felt that I was
supposed to write something to help others. But what? It became
clear to me a few years later when God started whispering about
what I must do.

During the pastor's sermon, I felt God whisper to me, not
audibly but in my heart, that I'd better pay attention to what He was
saying. I needed to start documenting how He talked to me and then
when He said so, to write a book about it. I thought, yeah, right ...
Who would believe me? Yet, as I reflected on God's words, I
concluded that if an ordinary person such as I could speak and listen
to God, then anyone could hear Him because God talks to each of us
all the time if we are aware enough to hear and listen to this ever-
present voice. Most people expect ministers to hear God. That's their
job, right? But I've learned that we can hear God talk if we open our

hearts and listen. So, I decided that I'd track in my journals the times He spoke to me, and later look back and see what became of His messages.

The pastor advised how to discern if the voice is truly God. He said there are three tests to consider. The first involved passing the scripture test. What is said should never contradict the teachings of the Bible. Second, what is heard should be put to the wisdom test. Would Jesus advocate it? And, third, ideas must be put to Godly counsel by asking trusted others if the words seem to be the voice of God or not.

Through the following stories, you will see how God spoke to me on numerous occasions and in a variety of ways. In the storms of life, I sometimes heard God clearly. At other times, I fruitlessly tried to control my fate by adjusting my own sails. However, through all of the ebb and flow of the waves of life, you'll see through my stories how listening to God and having a relationship with Him eventually opened up a whole new world, one where I could feel peace and love even in the chaotic downpours that came.

In my younger years, I didn't realize that God was and is always with me, often carrying me as He whispers words of encouragement to cheer me on. In addition, I also didn't discern that God "speaks" through others, through dreams and through nature. He can speak through numbers, synchronicity, music, even through license plates, and of course, the Bible. He does not prevent the storms from happening in our lives, but He will help get us through them and use these storms to teach us something, to develop our character, and ultimately to bring us closer to Him. In the chaos of the storm when I am most uncomfortable, most afraid, most frustrated, I learned to stop resisting and instead, to rejoice as I had been given an awesome opportunity for growth. Growth? Yes, growth. I didn't ask for it, but as the saying goes, if challenges don't kill you, they will make you stronger — that is, if you listen to God along the way. People often claim that "God doesn't give you more than you can handle." That is not true. While I don't believe God gives us all our troubles, we will certainly have seasons where we get more than we can handle. The goal then should be to lean on God to trust Him and to ask Him to help us through the storms of life because God can handle any situation. God helps us best when we seek His words, listen, and talk to Him.

This book is about my personal journey in how developing a closer relationship with God and learning to listen to Him can provide guidance and comfort in life. I believe that the Holy Spirit lives within us and that God communicates to us through the Holy Spirit. Each of us can become sensitive to hearing God speak through the Holy Spirit. I want to be clear that I am not a theologian by any means. I use the word "God," yet someone else could interpret that to be the Holy Spirit, Jesus, or some other name. To me, I believe that the Holy Spirit is in each of us, yet, at the same time, all three are one.

You may be thinking, "I don't want to grow. I'm happy right where I am." I thought that way too. Yet somehow, I came to realize that if there's something I must learn or do in life, the same patterns will come my way, giving me the opportunity to learn a particular lesson. For me, right when I think I have my life all planned out, I am tossed into a new chaotic storm that I must weather to learn an essential lesson.

Let me start from the beginning when the seas were calm — or so I thought.

PART I: God's Intervention and Purpose for Our Lives

When the seas seem smooth, God will often create a tidal wave as He did with me. I always wanted to be an entrepreneur or a top advertising executive, but God had other plans. Along the way, there were indications as to what my innate purpose was, yet I ignored them until the same message was sent over and over through other people. He put certain people in my life — my favorite high school English teacher, my best college friend, Dan, and my grandma, as well as many others who all inspired me and said just the right things at just the right time to direct me on my course — a course that, once looking back, I can see He'd plotted all along.

Be aware — God will talk through others when necessary, and while it may appear to be just happenstance, it's not. Everyone we meet has an important role in our lives — some to help and inspire us, others to frustrate and challenge us for growth. They all have a purpose.

My journey to figure out how and when to listen to my heart resembled Siddhartha's famous journey to enlightenment. The novel, Siddhartha, by Hermann Hesse recounts the self-discovery of a man named Siddhartha during the time of the Gautama Buddha. He knew that teachers and guides couldn't tell him what to do — that his purpose in life had to be found on his own. I, too, would have to figure out my life's purpose by listening to the Holy Spirit within me, guiding me. Figuring out your purpose can just be a matter of quieting yourself, so you can listen to your heart. This is another way God whispers.

Chapter 1: My First Time Hearing God Speak

It is important that we know and hear God's voice, for the words of God reveal the will of God.

—Larry Lea

It was my senior year of high school, and similar to many confident seniors, I pretty much had life figured out. Like a kindergartener, anxious, yet eager to leave for school, I couldn't wait to leave my parents' nest to go to UW-Madison where I would earn my degree in business and advertising. And, with life all planned out, I intended to move to Oregon to work for Nike where I would write new and improved slogans that would inspire thousands, maybe millions of athletes to "just do it." I took every business class offered in high school, was active in the Future Business Leaders of America club, and always had a job. I liked to make money. Ever since my first rummage sale at the age of three, I have loved bartering with people. If someone offered me a lower dollar amount for an item, I'd give them ten reasons why they should pay even more than my asking price. My strong persuasive skills made me think I was destined for success in the business world. I had everything planned out accordingly until April of my senior year when I had what was supposed to be routine surgery to remove four impacted wisdom teeth.

While in the surgery room as I lay helplessly sprawled out like some lab experiment, I heard the incompetent and disheveled surgeon panic as he told the nurse he hadn't given me the full dose of anesthesia because I had extensive nasal congestion. I guessed he wanted to make sure I was awake in case I started to choke. Nice. Well, with less anesthesia, I not only heard the nightmare of the drill — which sounded like bombs exploding in my mouth — but I also felt each of these painful terrorist attacks.

In the most pain I ever felt, I screamed, cried, and choked. I pleaded, "Please, God, if you really exist, please stop this stupid oral surgeon, or let me die. I can't take much more pain. Please, please, stop it now." The sound of the rattling drill paralyzed me.

"Hurry," the surgeon impatiently yelled at his nurse. "Get some air on her. Shoot, we're going to have to start CPR. Hurry, we're losing her." As I choked on my own blood and suffocated in the process, I quickly escaped from hell on Earth.

Looking down at my body, I stared confused at the crew who frantically tried to save me. Where was I? Why was I seeing the doctors work on me? The next sixty seconds felt like an eternity as I floated peacefully like a ghost above them. At that moment, I realized my private prayer had been answered: I gave God a challenge. He answered immediately, and I died. The pain of the drill rattled every bone in my body, breaking my spirit tooth by tooth. When I died, though, the pain ended abruptly. It felt like a huge victory as I overcame the terrorism in my mouth.

As my soulful existence left the surgeon's office, I bathed in the awe-inspiring bright white light of love. Earthly words just don't exist to describe this, but I'll do my best to paint the picture: I felt an overwhelming peacefulness that all was right in the world, that nothing could disturb the serenity created by the rainbows and spiritual auras that surrounded me. As I whizzed through a tunnel at a speed unknown to man, I saw quick glimpses of all the people who were important to me, both alive and dead ... my family, my closest friends, my pets, as well as the people of the future who I later learned would play a vital role in my life. Seeing these people showed me that everyone who came into my life, even for a second, was purposeful, meant to be, and could teach me something. Author Angel Flonis Harefa once said, "There will always be a reason why you meet people. Either you need them to change your life, or you're the one that will change theirs." These random encounters are not coincidences but rather part of God's plan.

My mind knew seeing people in the middle of surgery was strange, but I blamed the drugs in my system, reasoning that they gave me a weird but vivid dream. Real or not, I couldn't help but wonder how any of them would shape and influence my life. I could feel that all the individuals I encountered through my journey in the tunnel loved me unconditionally. Their love radiated joy in my soul.

I'll never forget one guy I saw from my future; he was a tall, dark, handsome, tan man, about six feet tall and 185 pounds with an athletic build — the epitome of hotness. He looked a little like Ben Affleck on whom I'd always had a crush; I wished so much that I would have had the chance to meet the Ben Affleck look-alike. At the end of the tunnel and toward the bright white and yellow light stood a silhouette. A loving parental voice who I somehow knew in my soul said, "Go back. It's not your time. You must go back. You have much to do." I felt nothing but love and warmth from this silhouette and knew with confidence that was Jesus talking to me.

"What? What am I supposed to do?"

"Just listen to your heart," He said.

"Is it really that easy?"

"Life isn't easy, but if you listen to your heart, which is filled with the Holy Spirit, you'll always find the answers that you need within you."

"But I like it here," I said, not knowing where I was exactly. I felt pure love and a level of complete relaxation that made me feel as if I floated on some gentle waves. Stress and drama didn't exist. It was how I felt with those who accepted and loved me unconditionally. It was comfortable, how life and relationships were supposed to feel. "How do I listen to my heart?" I asked Jesus.

"You will know. Now go back; you have one tooth left to take out, and I will make sure you do not feel pain," Jesus assured me. I wanted to talk more, but I left abruptly after I nodded to say I would go back and trust God. As I abruptly returned to my body, I coughed up blood and gasped for air as if my life depended on it.

Back in the surgeon's office, I heard the doctor say with a shaky, nervous voice, "You have only one tooth left. Hang in there. You're breathing just fine again, and we're almost done."

At home recovering after surgery, I remained quiet for a few days about this encounter as I didn't know if what happened was real, a dream, or even some strange April Fool's Day joke. If I told others this story, I knew they would be waiting for the punch line. But, over the course of the next few days, the nurse called a few times to check in. Finally, after the third phone call, my mom came over to me on the sofa, looking confused, and said, "Do you remember anything from your surgery?"

"Ummm, yeah, why?"

"Well, the nurse said you may have stopped breathing in the middle of it. I just can't believe that would happen in a standard wisdom teeth surgery."

"Really? You mean that wasn't a dream!" I said, trying to make sense of everything.

"Wait. What happened? What do you remember?" Mom asked, concerned and impatient.

"Well, the pain was so unbearable, and I asked God that if He was real to end the pain."

"Wait, you questioned if God was real?" Mom asked. I wasn't surprised that this was what my mom asked me about because she just isn't the type to get phased over stories of tunnels and bright lights. Her faith is strong.

"Um, yeah. You would too if you had so much pain and were desperate for it to end."

"Okay, okay. What happened next?"

"So I quickly went through a tunnel, saw you all upset in the waiting room, saw my best friend Amy fighting with her boyfriend, and then saw some of our relatives who died, smiling and opening their arms to me. Grandma and Grandpa Nekas said to tell Dad that they are fine and very proud of him."

"You saw Grandma and Grandpa? Wow!" she interrupted. "Okay, sorry. Keep going."

"I also think I saw people from my future who I don't know yet. And then I saw a figure that looked and felt like Jesus at the end of a tunnel with bright yellow glowing light. I felt intense love — lots of it. Jesus said to go back and that it wasn't my time. That I have more to do. That I must listen to my heart. I swear it all felt real. But this sounds crazy, and I figured it had to be a dream."

"The nurse said you stopped breathing because you choked on your blood from the surgery and couldn't breathe through your nose."

"Really?" I asked.

"Yes, and I can't believe that doctor did the surgery anyway. I knew we should have waited a few months and made an appointment with the surgeon who had a good reputation. I never heard of this guy and thought it was strange that he had an opening so quickly."

"Why were you upset in the waiting room when I thought I

saw you?" I asked.

"I heard you screaming out in unbearable pain and asked the receptionist if you could feel it. She assured me that all patients scream during surgery, but that since you were out, you wouldn't feel or remember anything."

"Well, I felt it all. It was horrible. I don't ever want to hear a drill again."

"You're never having work done by that surgeon again. I'm so grateful you came back. This is definitely a unique situation, but I've read of others who died, went through a tunnel just like you described. They were changed afterwards. You do have a purpose. Believe that," Mom reassured me.

"I hope you're right. Jesus said I'm supposed to listen to my heart, but Mom, I don't know what my heart says about what I am to do in the future," I pleaded.

"Give it time. I'm sure you'll know in time," she said.

The premonitions from my near-death experience came like someone playing a movie of my life in my head. I still get premonitions and prophetic dreams, and I now know they are whispers from God, trying to encourage and lead me on the right path. God's words to "listen to my heart" still speak to me today. The year God said those words, whether it was in person like I thought or some crazy dream, the band Roxette had a hit song called "Listen to Your Heart." Years later, that song still seems to miraculously come on the radio as a reminder to always listen to God's whispers. God knows that song will get my attention.

Some reading this may be thinking that this is a unique experience that happened to me, but the truth is that God whispers to everyone, not always audibly, but spiritually, to those who will listen. He may be trying to get your attention right now; he yearns for a relationship with you and wants to help guide you through your life storms. If you don't have storms now, it's just a matter of time before you do. Unfortunately, the sea of life doesn't remain calm for very long.

Chapter 2: Purposeful Encounters Guide Life

Certain people encounter our life at the perfect time for the most beautiful reasons, and you know right away it was a gift from God.
— *Brigitte Nicole*

Everyone, if lucky, can usually point to at least one influential teacher in his or her life. Mine came in an unexpected way. At the start of my senior year, I met Mrs. Cantwell, a spunky woman in her late fifties with shiny white and silver hair, a few wrinkles from the students who probably stressed her out over the years, and a no-nonsense attitude that basically said, "Don't mess with me." On the first day in her Advanced Composition class, I confidently told her, "I have you for two classes —this and journalism."

"Good. I can flunk you twice then," she replied without even a smirk on her face, which made me wonder if she was not joking.

"Um, you don't know who I am. I'm basically a straight A student," I said, defending my reputation.

"And you don't know who I am; I basically ruin people's GPA's."

I didn't respond but felt more determined than ever that I would prove her wrong. After a few weeks of class, she saw me in the hallway one morning. "Chris," she said.

I hated when she shortened my name like that. "It's Christine."

"Oh, yeah, sorry. I read your paper." Dramatic pause. "Yeah?"

"Well, I think you're going to be okay," Mrs. Cantwell said. "Okay? You mean it's good?"

"Oh, I didn't say that," Mrs. Cantwell said, but this time with a slight smile on her face.

The rest of the year, we bantered back and forth like that, but I learned that was just her way — her way of showing she cared.

After my near-death experience, Mrs. Cantwell caught me off guard again with her natural intuitiveness when she said, "You know that you will one day become an English teacher. It's what you're meant to do. Listen to your heart." My jaw dropped as she said those words — not just because she said I'd be an English teacher, but because she used the same four words that God did about listening to my heart.

In shock, I ignored the fact that she said to "listen to your heart" and replied jokingly, "No, I'd like to make money — thank you very much. Teachers are underpaid." Saying that always got under her skin because she probably knew I was correct, and I found it humorous to push her buttons.

"You won't be teaching for the money but because you're called to do it."

Her words secretly haunted me after that. Did she know something about me that I didn't? Growing up, I always played "teacher" with all my stuffed animals and loved to help my little brother, who was seven years younger, learn. In my senior yearbook, my peers shocked me by naming me "most likely to become an English teacher." I guess hidden in my heart, part of me always wanted to be a teacher, but you couldn't have even paid me to admit that then. Even though I respected my teachers, I just didn't think the profession was meant for me.

In fact, once I started college at the University of Wisconsin-Madison, I majored in business as planned. Fortunately, while attending, I made several good friends. One friend, who walked with a little waddle of excitement in his step and who lit up a room with his super white smile, seemed extremely special from the moment I met him. His name was Dan, yet we all nicknamed him Smiley Dan. When we talked, his hazel eyes listened intently, telling me that I was all that mattered at that moment. Not many people bother to put others first like that, especially now as we often "connect" through our phones and social media. The moment our eyes met, I knew in my soul that I saw him before. And then, my mind raced back to my journey through the tunnel. Oh my — I had that déjà vu feeling that I saw Dan when I died. Back in the tunnel, I must have had a glimpse of his face. I saw many faces but couldn't remember most of them until I saw them in real life. I knew immediately with every fiber of my being that Dan would play an instrumental role in my life. My body shivered with goose bumps at this realization, and I knew with all my heart that Dan and I were meant to be best friends.

I am proud to say that I became well-known among my group of friends for giving Dan his nickname "Smiley". It didn't take me too long to name him either — approximately two days of being around him, in fact, and the name, along with his pearly whites and radiant smile, just made sense. I still can't understand it, but the guy always had a smile on his face; his positive attitude, love, laughter, and happiness pulled others in like a magnet. I never heard anyone say a bad word about him. People couldn't. If they did, something would have been seriously wrong with them.

Dan accepted just about anyone — from the odd fellow on State Street, preaching about some New Age religion, to the unique person such as me. I'm sure that's why we clicked. I'll never forget when Sam was the last person I wanted to accept into our group of friends. Sam sported thick glasses with comb-over hair. Much like a scientist concentrating on his newest theory or invention, he often talked with his eyes closed and back slouched. We used to joke that his spazz-like moves when he danced resembled what a monkey might do on drugs with his arms flailing in all directions. Sam often wore the American flag — not the real flag, but he had a workout jumpsuit that was red, white, and blue, and whenever we saw him, it made us want to salute him. At times, we did just that and laughed to ourselves as we did so. To make matters worse, Sam had a crush on me, which made me want to avoid him like the plague. Years later, when I grew up, I felt remorse for how superficial it was to secretly make fun of him like that.

Dan sternly said to me, "Any friend of mine will be a friend of yours. You must give him a chance, especially since you don't really know him."

Over time, I did just what Dan said. Sam became a dear friend who brought many sincere laughs just like Dan did. And my friendship with Sam taught me never to judge people so quickly.

Dan wasn't just loving and accepting, but his sense of humor resembled Robin Williams at times. He often had me bursting at the seams with uncontrollable laughter — the kind where my body shook, my voice whined like I was having asthma attacks, and my eyes watered so much that it looked like I'd cried for days. Good times.

I'll never forget the time I had to study for a

psychology test, the type with those super tricky multiple-choice questions. You know the kind … the ones where you tried to figure out if the answer is A, B, C, D, E, both A and B or both B and C or A, B, and C, or all of the above or none of the above. By the time I finished reading the loaded question, I had to re-read it a few times just to figure what the heck the professor asked. When Dan desperately wanted me to come to a "Christmas in March" party, I kept saying no because my nerdy side got the best of me as I desired a 4.0 G.P.A. in order to make it into the School of Education to earn my teacher's degree and "make a difference in the life of a child," as the saying went. That's what I kept reminding myself. I now "listened to my heart" by majoring in English Education like God, Dan and Mrs. Cantwell encouraged me to do.

Yes, it's true — I switched my major from business to education at the very last moment when a major had to be declared. It was weird how that happened. A magnetic energy made me gravitate toward certain friends who majored in teaching. Somehow, I landed summer jobs that involved teaching high school students computer skills as well as coaching kids in basketball. When the time came to declare my major, I still felt in denial that teaching was what I wanted to do with the rest of my life, yet at the same time, I enjoyed the teaching roles I had previously. Looking back, the decision reminded me of Robert Frost's poem, "The Road Not Taken". Like the two roads in the poem that Frost claimed were equal, I wanted to save my plan of going into business for another day just in case the teaching path was not the correct one. Because both paths felt equal to me, I feared I'd make the wrong choice. In the end, and with the fear of regret, I had to just trust my gut and decide. It really seemed like suddenly, I became a teacher — a decision that still surprised me decades later, yet these actions support the idea of how we all have a soul's purpose. We are each here to do specific things in life, and when we allow our hearts and minds to align with God's intentions, we will know we are on the right path.

Back to my Christmas in March story and Dan's demand that I abandon studying and come. "I'm not asking you to get a root canal; I am asking you to come to one stinkin' party." After twisting my arm and offering me free pizza, which was always a good bribing device, I reluctantly went with him. To our horror, the party did not meet UW-Madison party standards.

"You dragged me away from studying to take me to a dry party?" I gasped with disbelief.

"Oh, c'mon. The party isn't too bad. We're getting practice for all those stupid high school dances we'll have to chaperone someday when we're real teachers and must act responsibly."

Smiley Dan was studying to be a high school math teacher. I often felt sorry for him as I wondered how on earth anyone could make teaching numbers exciting. With literature, I could at least tell stories and show movies. I always teased him that people only needed to know a little math to balance their checkbooks and figure out their finances. With the massive debt that so many people were in, including our nation's leaders, I let him know that today's math teachers failed civilization. He laughed and assured me that he'd change that.

At other parties, Dan acted as a detective by always keeping his eye on me and by keeping track of how many guys hit on me each night. With his list of guys who hit on me in hand, he called me "The Heartbreaker" or "One date Christine." I laughed it off, but knew he was right — I was picky about whom I dated, and most guys didn't see a second date with me. And Dan always laughed at how I never really became drunk. I never had to because if you knew me, you would know that I'm fun and wild enough as my sober self.

Dan teased me that I had to stay sober so I could keep track of which guy was which at various parties. And, when I dated three different Andys in a row and sometimes at the same time, all of whom were Scorpios, to make matters worse, life became even more interesting. A Scorpio, one of the twelve signs of the Zodiac, is born between October 23 and November 22. That alone was not the problem. Their sign, according to astrology, says that Scorpios are "introspective, reflective, mysterious, vengeful, calculating, and possessive." The fact that they are often introspective and reflective was no problem, but the other qualities listed were not pleasing or complementary to me.

For awhile, we referred to the men as Andy #1, Andy #2, and Andy #3. We always had a good laugh as Andy #2 called me once after a single date, saying, "You are my soul mate and the woman of my dreams." Needless to say, that was the end of Andy #2. And when Andy #3 sent me a dozen roses for my birthday with a heartfelt poem about how I should "frolic in my youth," after one date, that was the end of Andy #3. When I met a fourth Andy at a party, Dan banned me from dating him, saying that three men named Andy was enough to keep track of. Any more Andys would be much too confusing for him. As you can see, Dan basically took on the role as my dating agent. After that point, I never dated another Andy as they always brought too much trouble for me.

Of course, Dan had dates of his own. I'll never forget when he dated Trina, the girl who could put two tennis balls in her mouth. How one would figure out how to do that, I'll never know. Anyhow, Trina tried to befriend me — guess she knew she had to if she were to get anywhere with Dan. It must have been after the third date that she told me she was going to marry Dan one day and that I'd be a bridesmaid. I spit out my entire drink as I coughed and choked. "What? My Dan? You think you're going to marry Dan Tietz? Seriously?" She told me not to tell him.

A few minutes later, I pulled Dan to the side and congratulated him on the "big news" of how I would be in his wedding.

"What wedding?" For a second, he seemed to believe he and I were going to get married.

"Your wedding to Trina, silly."

"You're crazy."

"No, she thinks the two of you are going to get married. Do you feel that way about her?" I secretly did not want him to really like her or anyone else for that matter because that would put a dent in my future plans with him.

"No. She told you this?"

"Yes. I'm not supposed to tell you, of course, but you'd tell me if the situation were reversed," I replied.

"No, you needed to tell me. Thanks."

Like the calm after a thunderstorm, a sense of relief engulfed me after Dan told me they broke up that night. You may be wondering why I didn't date Dan since he was obviously such a good catch. Don't think I didn't consider it. That reminded me of another time my great friend Tori, my college roommate and also a close friend of Dan's, and I did a three-way call to him, except he did not know I listened on the other line. I know that was sneaky, but I was young and immature. Besides, I planned on telling him about this. Honest I did. It all started out as a joke as Tori asked Dan what he thought of me.

"What do you mean?" Dan asked.

"Um, well, you two are best friends, and friends make good couples. Why don't you two date? It seems like you get jealous when she has a boyfriend, or some new Andy pursues her. From my point of view, she doesn't like it when you have a girlfriend. Why not just admit you like her and get on with it?" Tori pushed.

"Well, I would like to date her one day. She's the type to marry. But I would not want to date her now as I'm not ready for something so serious. Our friendship means too much, and I would be bummed if something happened to it. Maybe later in life though. Yes, definitely later."

My heart beat a thousand beats per minute as I broke into a sweat with his declaration of future love. As I practically fell to the floor while I heard his response, I almost gave away that I listened intently to his every word. He echoed my heart's song, and as a result, guilt confronted my soul for tricking him and for knowing his inner heart without his consent. I think that must be how Romeo felt hearing Juliet's confession of love when she was on the balcony and didn't know he listened to her private musings.

After graduating UW-Madison and coming back to visit Dan, who was in his fifth year at college, my daydreams came to an end as I saw the rickety white house with chipped paint — 4812 Mifflin Street, Dan's house in Madison. As Dan greeted me by my car, he commented on my messy, cheap highlights.

"You're special, Christine. Your hair is a mutation. It's not blonde or brown."

"Gee, thanks. Good to see you too." But who couldn't laugh at that? Seriously, my yellowish, orangey looking highlights were the best I could afford on a beginning teacher's salary of a measly $22,000 per year. We went to our favorite bar, State Street Brats, where along with thousands of other Badger students, we kissed the moose on our 21st birthday. We ordered the famous 1994 Rosebowl drink, the one known for its six different fruity shots — a drink that still exists to this day! Don't think there's much in that drink besides that, which was totally okay after the past few weeks of teaching I had.

"Ahhhh, feels good to relax," I said as I took a sip of the Kool-Aid-like alcohol.

"What's wrong? You don't seem yourself. Aren't things getting better?" Smiley asked.

"No, not really. Can you believe they gave me a job in January without any curriculum, notes, or lesson plans for that stupid mythology class? I don't know what I'm teaching, which makes me feel as though I'm always pulling B.S. from the sky. It's not fun. I feel like I'm in the middle of a storm — lost and confused."

"Oh, I know what you mean. I feel that way sometimes in my student teaching, but I'm sure over time, you'll get more comfortable with what you're teaching them," he reassured me. "There's always a calm after the storm. All new things are hard at first."

"It's not just the curriculum. It's the students, the other teachers, the administration, the city of Menasha, the Fox Valley, the state of Wisconsin. Everything. The seniors in that stupid mythology class are always testing me. I hate it. This snotty senior girl named Jackie stood up the other day and told me that this has always been a blow off class, and that I better learn to ease up."

"What did you do next?" Dan asked.

"Well, then they asked me what mythology is, so I threw the question back to her. But it backfired as the students knew darn well that I don't know what I'm doing or that I don't even know what mythology is. Can you believe that I had to get some Cliff Notes to find out?"

"Well, you can't know everything," Dan tried to console me.

"But I should know what I'm teaching. Here, I went to one of the best colleges around, and I don't know anything about mythology. Wasn't college supposed to prepare me? How will I possibly get along in life not knowing anything about mythology? And you know what? I couldn't care less about Greek or Roman Gods. Whoever invented these tales must have been in their own fantasy world. Seriously, I'm just a gerbil going round and round, wasting energy in a cage, not really getting anywhere day after day," I said quickly, trying to get out all my frustration.

"Christine, you have to believe in yourself. They would not be teenagers if they didn't question and test you; they live for these moments. You'd do the same if you were them."

"True, but it still sucks," I pleaded.

"Be strong. Don't forget how the kids loved you when you student taught. Just keep trying and doing what you know is good for them, even if they continue to complain and hate you for it. Some of them will thank you later."

"Ugh. Maybe. I just can't wait until summer."

Just before I left, Smiley said, "Don't forget the lesson you learned from your near-death experience. You're meant to be a teacher. Listen to your heart — remember?"

I chuckled. "Yeah, I remember...how can I forget? Thanks, Smiley." I kept Dan's words of encouragement close to heart, and as I continued to drive home, I couldn't help but contemplate Smiley Dan's reminder of how I was meant to be a teacher.

My daydream was interrupted as I approached my driveway, and with perfect timing, the song "Listen to Your Heart" played on the radio again — a sign for sure. *Okay, God. I get it. I'll stay with teaching at least for a bit. Well, at least for one more year. But, God, please don't let me be poor all my life.*

Chapter 3: Prophetic Last Words

It is during our darkest moments that we must focus to see light.
—Aristotle

As I walked in the door from my weekend excursion with luggage and mail in my hand, the familiar brrrrinnngg of the land line phone blared.

"Where have you been?" Mom asked furiously.

"We have lots of news to tell you," Dad added. "For the past week, Grandma hasn't been able to go to the bathroom. They found a tumor blocking her intestines. Unfortunately, the doctors feel that they can't operate on it because it is terminal. It's just a matter of time before the cancer spreads."

"What?" I asked, shocked, thinking of how she seemed healthy when I saw her just a few short months ago. With tears in my eyes, I quickly asked, "How long does she have?"

"We don't know," Dad said sadly.

Two days later, I hesitantly and nervously left for my first master's residency at Northeastern University held at Martha's Vineyard. I hoped to grow as a writer and teacher as I majored in Writing. At first, I didn't want to leave because of Grandma's health, but then I remembered Smiley Dan encouraging me that this would be an awesome opportunity to spend time writing near the ocean as I thought about teaching and life. I reminded myself that Grandma wouldn't want me to sit home worrying about her. Knowing I made the right decision to come to the Vineyard, I wrote Smiley Dan a postcard:

Dear Smiley,
I've met lots of good people here at the Vineyard, and I'm getting many new teaching ideas. I learned today about how to motivate students with a reader response approach to teaching. I'm starting to believe in a chaos theory with a Socratic Seminar. People learn best when what they know to be true is challenged. Remember Bloom's Taxonomy — the classification system used to define a person's thinking, learning, and understanding

through different levels of question techniques? I think that needs to be rewritten. I'll create my own theory of how students learn when questioned. Maybe these ideas will help me with that mythology class I told you about. Nothing can hurt, hey? I hope you're having fun in Badger land and are not partying too hard without me! Miss you and see you soon.

Love,
Christine

As my first summer residency at grad school ended, I hustled back to my hometown in Wisconsin, anxious to visit family and friends whom it felt like I missed for years, rather than a few months. I worried about Grandma's health, my only grandma left. I raced against time to have one more chat with her and one more hug. Immediately after arriving home, I drove two hours to Grandma's house in Illinois, thinking I could catch up with my friends later.

As I drove, I thought about how I couldn't wait to catch up with Dan, but a disturbing vision popped into my head: Dan rode his motorcycle, speeding around a curve on a country road, and as he did so, a deer darted out in front of him, causing him to be spooked and lose control. I saw how he landed several yards away from his motorcycle, suffering severe head injuries. My eyes filled with tears, and I metaphorically shamed myself for thinking such a morbid thought. I couldn't understand why I'd imagine something like this. I felt a darkness and deep depression in my soul like I never experienced before. As I continued to drive, I reassured myself that my mind was just playing tricks on me. After all, exhaustion dripped from my pores as I flew home the night before, and with the anxiety over Grandma's health status, the stress spread heavy like a thick fog. I yearned to see the sun. Both Grandma and Dan were bright stars in my life, and I prayed a quick prayer that they'd both be shining for a long time.

As I happily sauntered into Grandma's house, she sat up abruptly with a radiant glow and sparkle of excitement in her crystal blue eyes.

"Well, look who's here."

I darted to her and hugged her warmly.

"So, how was the Vineyard?"

"Good," I responded, not really knowing how to elaborate.

"What did you write about?"

"Oh, you know ... the usual, writing about writing, and my philosophy of teaching both reading and writing — boring stuff like that. But I did come up with a chaos theory about how to teach literature. Basically, it's good to shake things up so that kids are challenged to learn. We only learn in the challenges and often when we are completely lost and confused."

"Oh, I see. Your theory sounds like you could apply it to life. Well, it's so good to see you again," she announced with a cheery voice.

Apply my theory to life? I didn't fathom how at the time. Concerned with how time visiting Grandma always flew by so quickly, especially since we were both so skilled at talking, I just wanted to take time and save it in a bottle, especially when the future seemed like a massive sea with no clear docking point. I had no control, but then, did I ever really? Both the idea of having control and time were illusions, not reality.

After seeing Grandma on the road to recovery, my spirit slightly uplifted, yet that strange image of my vision with Dan getting hurt kept popping up in my mind. Why? Why was I thinking that Dan would get in an accident? I hated the pit in my stomach that I continued to feel. I couldn't wait to get home to call Smiley Dan. When I finally called around 5 p.m., I was so bummed that he wasn't home. Things weren't like today when everyone has a cell phone and can be reached at any moment, 24-7. I heard his happy voice on the answering machine and said after the beep, "Hi, Dan. I'm back in town. Give me a call. Can't wait to catch up. Oh, I had a strange feeling today. I had a vision that you're going to get into a motorcycle accident. I know — crazy, but please go slowly and wear your helmet. I know it sounds stupid, but just in case, please do it. Remember how I sensed that Amy's dad had an aneurysm before I knew it was true? So, please be safe. Can't wait to talk to you and tell you all the crazy stories from the Vineyard. You'll need to go there sometime and check out Gay Head Town Beach. It has a nude section just for you. Ha, ha. Unfortunately, the people who are nude are not the ones you'd want to see. Talk soon."

Did I just say what I thought I said? A motorcycle accident? Did I actually tell him that? Again, I was not sure where that thought came from, but I learned to trust my gut even with negative news. The morning's vision of Dan replayed in my mind again. Surely, that was just a scary no-nonsense daydream, yet I warned him to wear his helmet, thank God.

Next, I called my best friend, Amy, with whom I'd been friends since we were both three. I tried to explain to her my scary premonition, hoping she'd believe me. I couldn't shake my strange dream. All day long, something deep inside me felt that the essence of time wasn't linear, that the future had been predetermined, and on some sacred level, the angels whispered to my subconscious that my life would never be the same again. Against my common sense, for that moment in time, I saw the future not literally, but figuratively, and I knew I picked up on some form of energy that happened in real time, something I could not quite grasp. As my body jittered and shook, somewhere deep inside, I knew this to be true. With all my heart, I wanted to ignore the deep melancholy that felt like someone I loved passed on. But, my entire body continued to fatigue and for no known reason, my soul continued to cry helplessly like a piece of me had been smothered to death; I could not ignore or trick fate even though I desperately wanted to. With each passing hour, my heart continued to break into tiny pieces. I didn't understand. Confusion invaded my mind and heart like a steady tide.

Years later, my research on time helped to shed light on why I felt that the future was the present. The one and only Albert Einstein said, "Time has no independent existence apart from the order of events by which we measure it." Einstein concluded in his later years that the past, present, and future all exist simultaneously. In 1952, in his book *Relativity,* he discussed Minkowski's Space World interpretation of his theory of relativity where Einstein wrote, "Since there exists in this four-dimensional structure [space-time] no longer any sections which represent 'now' objectively, the concepts of happening and becoming are indeed not completely suspended, but yet complicated. It appears, therefore, more natural to think of physical reality as a four-dimensional existence, instead of, as hitherto, the evolution of a three-dimensional existence."

Einstein's belief in an undivided solid reality was clear to him, so much so that he completely rejected the separation we experience as the moment of now. He believed there is no true division between past and future, but rather a single existence. To put it simply, another philosopher, Alan Watts said, "I have realized that the past and future are real illusions, that they exist in the present, which is what there is and all there is."

While I tried to explain to Amy my melancholy feelings about the past and present regarding Dan, the unwelcome beep of the phone interrupted our conversation. I switched over to a new caller.

"Hi, Christine ... This is Tori's mom calling," she said. I couldn't help feeling confused as to why she called me at 10 p.m. on Wednesday night but knew that Tori was driving to her parents to get ready for her upcoming wedding and thought that maybe her mom had some details related to that. Tori couldn't call me herself while on the road as this was before people had cell phones. "I have some bad news," Tori's mom said as she started crying and then found the courage to stutter out, "Dan was killed tonight on his motorcycle."

Not believing what I just heard, I yelled at the top of my lungs, "What! Not MY friend, Dan. No, not MY Dan. You mean that he's hurt, not dead, right?" That's impossible, I thought. It never ever occurred to me that he could die, and even though I had a crazy daydream of this happening, I didn't really believe it. He and I were supposed to get married one day although neither of us consciously knew that, but it's funny how my soul decided to shout the truth out in a time of crisis.

"I'm sooo sorry," she expressed with a shaky voice as she cried uncontrollably with me on the phone.

Feeling punched in the stomach a thousand times, I could hardly breathe. "Noooooo," I hysterically screamed and somehow muttered the words that he was supposed to call me back. He will call me back — I kept telling myself. I warned him to wear his helmet! "How can this be true?"

She tried to explain, but my mind ran a thousand miles per hour with hundreds of simultaneous images and memories of good times with my best friend, Dan.

Stumbling and falling to the ground in a foggy gaze, I looked at my favorite picture on my mantel of Dan and me at the Christmas in March party, not believing what I just heard. I clicked over to Amy and screamed at the top of my lungs, crying, screaming, crying, screaming.

Hysterical, I gasped for breath as hot sweat dripped over my body. I wanted to die. I wanted to be with Dan wherever he was. I couldn't go on without him.

"Oh my God. Oh my God. Oh my God," I shouted as I

continued to cry helplessly like someone just stabbed my heart.

"What? Tell me what's going on. You're scaring me," Amy insisted.

I tried to get the words out as I started to hyperventilate again and almost fainted from shock. "He's ... he's ... he's ... dead ... Oh, my God. Help us!"

"Who?"

"Daaaaaan," I cried.

"What? How?"

"Oh my God ... Dan ... my Dan ... on his motorcycle, just like I dreamed. It's all my fault. I dreamt it, and it came true. I can never go to sleep again."

After hanging up the phone with Amy, I pounded the floor like a three-year old having a temper tantrum, and I threw all books in sight around my stuffy apartment, not caring what they hit or broke. My mind worked overtime. I couldn't breathe. I couldn't communicate. I could only scream as anger made me a wounded animal trying to escape.

This isn't fair. Why him? Why MY best friend? Why such a good person? Things like this shouldn't happen to good people. He was supposed to be in my wedding one day, or perhaps he was the one I would have married. He and I just discussed that fact a few months ago, the night of the 1997 Packer Super Bowl win. I'll never forget that conversation. He called and woke me up at midnight. He said he was going to break up with his girlfriend at the time, and then asked about us.

"What about us?" I asked, confused.

"Every time you date someone, or I date someone, it just doesn't work out. Maybe we should just date each other," Dan said matter-of-factly.

I laughed into the phone, not believing he actually said that. "How about we get married if we are both thirty and single?"

"Deal!" Dan said cheerily. "That's only six years away!"

That conversation proved to me that he did have feelings for me, but we were both not ready to act on them yet. *There would be plenty of time,* I thought.

It didn't matter now. He was gone. "Why, God? He was such a good math teacher. He was the one I could tell anything to. Who would I tell all my deepest and darkest secrets to now? Why, God? Why do this to the world? Take a bad person. Not him. Why, God?

Why? I don't understand. I never will."

Days later, as I searched for comfort, I wrote Grandma, who usually had some good wisdom to share. I had been writing to Grandma since I was in the third grade and bragged about all the pen-pals I had from all over the nation and world. Grandma said, "Why don't you write me? I live two hours away in Illinois and don't get to see you very often. That would be a fun way to stay in touch."

My pen pals often sent me scratch and sniff stickers while Grandma always sent a cute letter on light blue stationery with some inspirational advice or Bible verse that I didn't quite understand. We had been writing to each other every two weeks from when I was eight years old until I was twenty-four. It comforted me to write and get letters from Grandma as I knew she really cared and loved me. She was a second mom, and even though my mom had similar wisdom regarding life's universal challenges, it was sometimes easier to hear the truth from someone older and wiser. I respected Grandma and listened to her even in my stubborn moments.

Confronted with the tidal wave of grief, I wrote:

Dear Grandma and Grandpa,
I'm sure you've heard by now how my best friend Dan was killed on his motorcycle. We shared so many good times. He was actually the first friend I made at UW-Madison. We took most of our teaching classes together. He was the one I turned to with all my problems. He was one of the few who accepted me just as I am. From day one, he had me laughing. Nicest guy I ever met. You remember him, don't you? I'm sure you met him at my graduation party. It's not fair that he's gone. The pain is so great; I don't know how to deal with this. And I don't get God. Why would God take someone so young? I don't know if I believe that things happen for a reason like you always say. What reason could there be for his death? I wish I knew where Dan was and why this had to happen. Is he at peace? Is he with us spiritually? I need answers. Sorry, I have nothing positive to report. Well, I hope all is well with you. Talk more soon.

Love,
Christine

As the days lingered on, my emotional emptiness consumed me, and while I tried my best to keep busy, it was hard to do when a part of me just died. I looked with envy at other people who still had their close college friends. No, actually, I looked at them with bitterness. No one understood, even though they thought they did. People said stupid things like "I know how you feel. I lost my dog once." How dare they compare my best friend's death to that of a dog. Some others said how they lost their grandparents, so they knew what loss felt like. I could not help but think how someone who lived a full life was not the same as someone who died young. No one understood. I lived in my own dark tornado and couldn't find the eye of the storm where calmness was supposed to be. Everything I touched and everything I did became swept up by the tornado's grip. Beyond angry with God, it would take years before I'd trust him again. I felt betrayed. Like someone with a middle school mentality, I did not want to be friends with God because he took my best friend. Two weeks after Dan's death and funeral, I received a familiar letter from Grandma on light blue stationery with a daisy border:

Dear Christine,

At our age, we have lost so many close friends and relatives. It is not pleasant when that happens, but to some degree, expected. Death is a part of life, as you know.

Thank the Lord for sending a great friend like Dan into your life. You shared so many good times together, and now you still have all those lovely memories.

Time goes by so quickly. When you were born—my baby had a baby—life has a way of going on, no matter what. Hope you can have some "fun" days before we get our winter weather. Come see us any time. You are always welcome. We are doing okay—a day at a time.
                 Love,
                 Grandma and Grandpa

Yes, she was right; I had wonderful memories of Dan, but was it so wrong to want more? I expected more. Why shouldn't I have more? At 23 years old, the hands of death whisked him away. He only taught one year of high school math and had many more years to give the world. Just before I left for the Vineyard, I remember him saying, "Christine, I think I'm going to look for a new career. These students don't seem to care about math, and I don't feel I'm making a difference. I work so hard and feel I'm getting nowhere."

"Dan, that's nonsense. Don't you remember me saying the same thing my first year? The first year of teaching sucks! And it sucks for everyone! They forgot to tell us that in college. And all those idealistic teacher movies like *The Dead Poet's Society* give the false impression that we can save the world. We can't. Every lesson you do, you have to create from scratch unless there are some kind, veteran teachers who will give you some of their materials. You need to give it another year. And no teachers see results until the end of the year anyway."

"You really think so?"

"Um, yeah. I know so. Yep. You can't quit this soon," I tried to convince him.

I knew deep down that he would persevere through the madness of teaching his first year. But he was gone. It didn't matter now. It irked me that he never knew what a great teacher he really was.

At his funeral, over fifty of his students drove more than two hours to pay their respects. I kept thinking what a shame it was that he didn't know how he touched all those lives. As I realized we should always tell people how we feel while we're living, I felt guilty that I never told him of my secret crush on him, yet I believe now we both knew anyway. With Dan's death on my mind, I reflected on how Grandma also often discussed with me how she had to say goodbye to many of her friends due to cancer and other age-related issues. Grandma's friends died when they were older; that had to be a little easier to accept. Unfortunately, Grandma's positive advice didn't help me as I tried to grasp life by more than just the thread that I held onto with each day.

A day after Grandma's letter, fate sent me a strange and ironic postcard with a picture of the Wisconsin Badger from Smiley Dan that had been rerouted to me in Wisconsin from Martha's Vineyard. It read:

Dearest Christine,

*Thank you for the postcard. Hope you're doing well in
Martha's Vineyard. Does she serve lots of wine? Ha, ha. I'm
having quite a July, camping and partying with the guys (this
last weekend, we partied Thursday, Friday, and Saturday
nights) etc. All is going well, and I really miss your laughs
and smiles. Can't wait to see you soon.*

Love,
Dan

P.S. Like the postcard of my (our) home state? I do.

This postcard caught me off guard. Right when I thought I
would never hear from him again, fate surprised me. I looked at the
silly Badger on the front of the postcard and laughed. Then I cried at
the irony of being reminded of my home state when I was no longer
out of town. What strange force caused Dan to pick up a pen and
write? He was a math teacher, for crying out loud, and hated writing!
It's almost like he knew the future — that he was going to die and
needed to give me something to remember him by. Was he meant to
die when he did? Even though his energy slowly left this world and I
felt that, I knew I'd always be connected to him in some way. My
soul knew it. Not only did he write me, but he was sentimental, a
sentiment usually reserved for only birthdays and Christmas cards. I
held the postcard close to my heart and reread it a dozen times.
These were Dan's last words to me. I laughed hysterically because
he always had a way of getting the last word.

The hands of time crawled slowly for weeks. If it were not
for the routine of teaching to keep me grounded, my zombie-like
state would have been constant like time itself. Fate woke me once
again unexpectedly only a few months later on a beautiful October
day.

Since Grandma lived far away, I wanted to save gas money
and rode with my parents to visit. In the middle of the car ride, my
dad said abruptly, "Christine, you realize that Grandma is dying,
right? This is why she was moved to a nursing home a few days
ago."

"Whaaaaaaat? What do you mean?" I guess I had been in denial.

"Her major organs are starting to shut down, and when the kidneys go, you know it won't be much longer," Dad solemnly explained.

"But they have her on morphine, so she's comfortable," Mom added as if that extra piece of information was enough to take away the pain that pierced my heart once again.

I knew what Dad meant, but hearing her last moments were upon us woke me up, a reality check I didn't want to understand. Ignorance, of course, was bliss.

For the rest of the ride, no one said a word. What was left to say? My eyes gazed out the window as I daydreamed about the false alarm a few months before. Grandma said then that all would work out. I trusted this advice again. I couldn't help thinking that my parents were wrong. I wanted them to be wrong. The urgency they felt must be incorrect, I kept telling myself.

I took a deep breath as we started toward the nursing home, which was much different than the hospital Grandma was in last time she became ill. As I hesitantly walked into the depressing place, I noticed the helplessness of the residents. Many complained that they wanted to be moved. Some groaned to be fed. Others had no twinkle in their eyes, yet a look of utter loneliness permeated their aura. Some longed to be loved, to be touched, to be cared for. Most were in wheelchairs and walkers. One lady stared at me as I walked in as if she wished I were there to save her from hell. I looked back at this lonely lady and saw how she tried to walk out the door and escape, but the alarm woke everyone as she tried to do so. As I walked along the desolate hallway like a child wanting to protect myself from what else I might see, I couldn't help smelling the stuffiness and age of the building. And then it hit me so hard that I wanted to run far away and cry like the child inside me. People who came here wasted away until they were gone. No wonder that lady wanted to escape as if she were in a prison. Just then, I started to worry for Grandma's sake.

With baby steps behind Mom and Dad, I took a

deep breath and gingerly walked into Grandma's musty old person's room. After one look at her, my eyes swelled, my cheeks became puffy, and I started to cry like a three-year old. Thankfully, she rested at the time, so she didn't see my pain. For the first time, I understood that death was near. Grandma's frail body was skeletal. Her usual rosy-red cheeks had a purplish-blue hue. Outside the room, blowing my nose, I gave myself a pep talk. I had to be strong; Grandma was, so I had to be too. Suddenly, I thought back to the recent letter she wrote me about how to deal with Dan's death. I realized she had been preparing me for her own, reminding me life goes on, and we needed to be thankful for the good times we had with those we love while they are here on Earth. Uninvited questions invaded my mind. If Grandma died, who would I write to? She explained Dan's death the best she could to me, but who would explain hers? I quickly convinced myself I didn't have time to worry about these questions now, so I boldly blew my nose one last time and marched into the room, pretending to be full of courage.

As I stood next to her while she slept like a little angel, I noticed her eyes started to flutter.

"What are you all doing here?" she mumbled. While her words were slurred from the morphine she was on, she was far from intoxicated as she understood everything going on.

Gently, I held her hand as I tried not to hurt her or hit any wires or buttons. With her glassy eyes and dazed look, she said sternly, "Don't worry about me. I'll be fine."

That was just like her—always trying to comfort me instead of just resting and taking care of herself. I sat in awe of her courage like any soldier ready and willing to accept the inevitable.

"I'll come again next week," I said after several minutes of not knowing what to say.

"Please, don't worry about me," she mumbled.

"I love you. Goodbye," I said with a few tears in my eyes.

Grandma nodded a little, and I could tell if she could have moved her muscles to smile, she would have. Looking me straight in the eyes with a tinge of sadness while her blood pressure continued to drop dramatically to levels close to death, Grandma said clearly, "Good-bye, Christine. Keep writing."

Goosebumps overcame my body as my soul spoke directly

with hers. She was still alive but barely hanging on, as a slight breeze permeated the room and another lonely tear fell silently on my cheek. At that exact moment, I knew with certainty that this was our last good-bye. I knew the sadness in my grandma's eyes was not for herself, but for me as she accepted her inevitable death. I knew her soul spoke to mine. And I knew these last words would always be a part of me. In this instance, I knew that God spoke through her, and realized whether I wanted to or not that I had to keep writing the book that God asked me years ago to write regarding how He speaks to all of us.

In our last conversation before I left the hospital room, I told her I'd come visit her next Saturday. When I arrived the following Saturday, I found her lying peacefully at rest in her casket. While I knew her death was imminent, one can't ever be fully prepared to say goodbye forever. To say I felt heartbroken all over again would be an understatement. With an empty soul, disappointment and much anger toward God, I lost my faith for two years. My relationship with God was like that of a father and a teenage daughter. God loved me unconditionally like a father would love a daughter, but my life turned upside down with the loss of Dan and Grandma, and so I blamed God for all the loss in my life. With bitterness and anger, I lived in a thick fog of deep depression during those years and didn't care about listening or talking to God.

After those first two years, my friends begged me for weeks to go to church with them. Reluctantly, and more because I wanted to go to lunch at a new restaurant in town afterward, I gave into going with them. At first, as I hesitantly walked into church, I wanted to run away because I felt like an intruder and automatically became annoyed when I heard the familiar hymn, "Amazing Grace" — the same song that played at both Dan's and Grandma's funerals. But then the pastor's words woke me up, softening my heart. The charismatic, young thirty-some year-old pastor said, "Just because you are a follower of Jesus does not mean your life will be easy or will go your way. Jesus always loves you and is there for you. Trust him." As I thought about how life did not go my way, tears dripped from my eyes in a matter of minutes, and I needed many tissues. Slowly, as I continued to open my heart and listen, peace overcame me as God's love wrapped around me like a blanket comforting me and making me feel at home once again.

After Grandma's death, I kept writing to Grandpa as he took on the role of my wise counselor, which was fun. He never had the chance to talk much since Grandma did most of the talking while alive. While the idea of writing a book on how God speaks sounded great, it didn't seem like God spoke very much, at least not to me, or maybe I couldn't "hear" anything. I kept asking Him to send me the right man to date and possibly one day marry, but the wrong guys kept knocking on my door. To wake me up to reality, God finally worked through my grandpa.

One Christmas, while my family played Texas Hold Em, my boyfriend, Luke, looked at me with disgust, saying, "You dork. I can't believe you played that card." Grandpa scowled as Luke belittled me. With the tone he used, Luke could very well have just said I was stupid. Luke's influence subtly changed me from a confident, no-nonsense lady to one who seemed meek and suffocated — not the real me at all.

The next morning as we ate our Cheerios, Grandpa surprised me, saying, "After praying about this, I feel like God and Grandma would want me to talk to you. I can't sit here and not say anything. Out of all sixteen grandkids, you remind me the most of Grandma. She was a strong, stubborn at times, but funny and loving woman. She would never let me talk to her like Luke spoke to you, calling you a dork. She'd throw it back or even throw her bowl of popcorn at me. If you're thinking of marrying Luke, you better think again, and be careful. From what I see, he doesn't build you up or bring out your best qualities. Instead, he belittles you and makes you self-conscious, and that's just not who you are."

"Oh, he's just joking, Grandpa." All my friends had tied the knot or were in the process of doing so, and I, too, didn't want to be single forever. In my mid-twenties, I worried that my eggs wouldn't last forever. I heard of women having infertility in their late twenties, and it didn't help that my parents awkwardly kept reminding me of that sad fact too. But Grandpa's words echoed in my soul every minute for several days. After a week of pondering Grandpa's thoughts, I realized that God had to talk through Grandpa because I just wasn't listening. There were clear signs and wake-up calls that Luke was not the one, but I had blinders on. I later realized that love can't be forced. That too is all a matter of God's will and perfect timing.

PART II: Love Lives Forever

The one thing that helped me mourn the loss of my best friend, Dan, and my loving grandmother was the realization that their love would never die. I'm grateful that their legacies, their memories, and their love for me are very much alive and always will be. They made an imprint that lives on well beyond their life-spans. I have faith that I will see them again when the time is right. Since I have some dreams and goals to achieve yet, I'm hoping that time is not too soon. Real love will have its challenges. In my story of finding my soul mate, I hit some serious waves head on right away and questioned whether I could stay afloat. As you will see, however, what is meant to be and what is real can never be torn apart. God provided me a chart on how to navigate the treacherous storms, and he will for you too if you seek and ask.

Chapter 4: Purposeful Reminders: Loved Ones Are with Us

What we have once enjoyed deeply we can never lose. All that we have loved deeply becomes a part of us.
— Helen Keller

Thinking over Grandpa's words and praying about the situation, I journaled all the ways that my relationship with Luke suffocated me. After I did so, I felt surprised and extremely disappointed that Grandpa was correct. I needed to listen to the truth as it became obvious that I had to let Luke go so that the door could be opened for real love. That night with sadness in my heart, I thought about how I wished I could find someone like Dan. And then, an angel came to me in my dreams, insisting that I wasn't alone. The angel showed me how all the people I love never left me because love and the memories of those we love live on within us. That realization made me smile and opened my heart a little.

A few weeks later, I saw a dead tree branch from a storm, yet the main part of the tree lived and reached up tall and proud, hopeful as it reached toward the bright sun. I pictured Dan as the broken off branch talking to me, the living part of the tree. From that image, this poem was born.

Advice For the Living—

Do not shed your leaves
or droop your branches
before your time.
Do not become a
dark, hollow tunnel.

Instead,
when the rain kisses,
drink.

Hug the rays of gold.
Sway with God's breezes.
Let the stars inspire.

And the birds' songs
free you.

Let your colors
dance in rainbows
on an autumn day.

Let the puffy white clouds
paint patterns of beginnings.

Reach out with your roots.
With each new ring of life,
remember and rejoice in the
layers of long ago.

And, as you remember,
know your tears
are not because I'm gone
but because I'm here with you.
Always.

And days, weeks, months, and even years later, Dan's spirit
continued to be with me. My first teaching job out of college landed
me in a small northern town in Wisconsin. This just happened to be
the same high school that both Dan and a few other close college
friends of mine graduated from. To be working with the teachers
who taught and inspired Dan was a unique experience as I often
asked them for stories to tease him. When he died, my colleagues
knew him well both as a person and as a student, so they understood
the magnitude of my loss, and were able to comfort me while I
grieved — a true blessing.

A year after Dan's death, a job opened close to where I grew
up in a suburban city near Milwaukee, in the same high school
where Dan taught math. I applied to the high school and surprised
myself in getting the job out of hundreds of applicants. Part of me
must have felt that by being close to those who knew him when he
died would make me feel better. It didn't, not even a little bit.
However, on one particularly stressful teaching day close to the
beginning of the school year as I searched through my desk drawer
for a marker, I instead found a picture of Dan and me from our

college days. It was our favorite "Christmas in March" party. The crazy thing, though, was that I didn't put the picture there. After discussing the incident with one of my work friends, Jean replied, "Well, that was Dan's classroom and desk, I think. You are teaching in the same room and must have the same desk he had."

"What? How can that even be possible? I teach English, and he taught math."

"Oh, well, after the school was remodeled this year, the English wing is now in the old math wing."

Dumbfounded, I smiled and knew this was purposeful synchronicity, rather than a simple coincidence, which served as a reminder that the memories of those we love will always live on. With this realization, my heart warmed with gratitude for this blessed friendship.

Chapter 5: Finding Love When Least Expected

Important encounters are planned by the souls long before the bodies see each other.
— Paulo Coelho.

For the next few years after Dan's and Grandma's death, I looked for love in all the wrong places. Perhaps I didn't give any man a fair chance as I compared all of them to Dan's fun, outgoing and loving personality. I really just wanted Dan's friendship back to fill the hole in my heart, and I convinced myself that no one I met would be good enough. Having just been burned by my past relationship with Luke, the last thing I wanted to do was be in one again, especially since I planned to move two hours away to take another new job in Illinois. I recently told God that if he wanted me to date again, he'd have to make it crystal clear because I had closed the door on love. Done. Done. Done. Done with dating and love. I was onto a new chapter. At that point, I only cared about hanging out with my girlfriends and having fun. In fact, Gloria Gaynor's song, "I Will Survive" became my new mantra.

With my ambition high and the worldwide open with opportunities, I decided to leave the school where Dan once taught and take a different teaching job two years later at a brand new high school where I'd have the unique chance to help train new teachers and teach all honors classes. One day in May, my friend Kristi called, begging me to go out. I didn't really want to. Not only did I sport a bad hair day, but I had a pimple the size of a mountain on my chin, as well as exhaustion from all the emotions of the job search and future change on the horizon. But she wouldn't let go of the idea of going to a March of Dimes benefit dance at the Milwaukee County Zoo. She continued to argue that since the local cover band, The Love Monkeys, would be playing, that in itself was reason to go out. Stubbornly, I told her that I just wanted to stay in my comfy black yoga pajamas, watching a *Dateline* special about some new murder mystery. Some guy killed his wife. It sounded just awesome and made me happy to be single.

After hanging up the phone with my friend, I resigned myself to stay in for the evening, but God spoke to me clearly,

"You really should go out tonight. Never know who you'll meet, and you always have fun listening to live music. It soothes your soul."

Annoyed at the clear message, I realized I had to go but didn't understand why. Like a child listening to her father, I dragged myself to meet my friends in the monkey section to listen. As the music blared from bands such as the Barenaked Ladies and Dave Matthews, my friend Kristi excitedly said, "That tall, dark, and handsome man with the red baseball cap and glasses keeps checking you out. Look!"

Me? Really? I thought. It couldn't be true with my frizzy hair and big friggin red pimple on my chin. No way would I hit it off with anyone that night. Despite my negative thoughts, I decided to look his way. As I did so, he quickly turned away trying not to get caught looking at me, which reminded me of middle school. I even glanced behind me to see if he was looking at someone else, but there wasn't anyone there. Okay, I could play this game. As the night swung on, I decided to just have fun and dance with my girlfriends. As I danced to the 80's music with my silly dance moves, including the lawnmower and the "Elaine" dance from the hit show *Seinfeld*, I accidentally bumped into the handsome fellow. Looking back, I think he purposely plotted to be by my side all along. The minute our eyes met, he smiled warmly and lit up the entire room. My mind in a trance flashed back to some familiar time. I saw him before. I just knew it. Could it be? Could it be? And then, just like that, I realized how I knew him. I saw him when I had my near death experience many years before. Wow. He really existed. He was here. Right now. I had flashbacks to seeing him in the tunnel and wished I knew him then. He interrupted my thoughts and flirtatiously asked, "How should I wear my hat?"

I couldn't help but laugh at such a stupid pick-up line. This guy must be a good one if that was the best he could think up. We danced, flirted, talked, and flirted some more. "What's a great girl like you doing single?" he asked as he tried to dance like Justin Bieber.

"No, you tell me first. Why are YOU still single?" I asked while he continued to try to impress me with his dance moves.

Phil replied confidently, "I'm looking for a solid, Christian girl who knows how to live life to the fullest. I just lost my best friend due to melanoma and realized how life is so short." We stopped dancing and walked over to a nearby table to continue talking.

Wow. He seemed too good to be true, yet our conversation was so natural. I loved how he talked about real life and not superficial stuff. I told him about Dan and the motorcycle accident, as well as how his death changed me too. After sharing stories, he gave me a slip of paper with his phone number on it, saying to call him. Still on my aloof kick with men, I proudly gave the piece of paper back.

"I'm sorry, but I don't call guys first," I said confidently, but secretly wondered why I played this hard-to-get game with a man whom I wanted to know from years before when I saw him in the tunnel.

"Well, what is your number then? I'll call you," he asked, a bit shocked. To me, it looked as if I might have been the first woman not to jump at an opportunity to date him.

I wrote my number on a wrinkled Leff's Lucky Town bar napkin. Phil took the number like a special treasure, folding it carefully and placing it in his wallet. As the evening went on, Peter Gabriel's song, "In Your Eyes," played. Just like in the movies, he looked lovingly in my eyes, kissed me, and spun me around.

"I don't kiss on the first date," I said.

"Good thing this is not a date then," he said, smiling.

Quick with the comebacks. I liked that. As he walked me to my car to say goodbye, he asked if I'd join him for 2 a.m. breakfast at George Webb, a routine he seemed to do often after going out.

"No thanks," I replied. The look of shock on his face stunned me. I knew then that he'd probably never been turned down by a girl before. Without hesitation, he gave me a last kiss goodnight.

"What are you doing?" I questioned.

"Marking my territory like the deer do when I hunt."

I burst out laughing. "You're weird," I replied.

"I'll call you," he insisted.

"I'll believe it when I see it. Goodbye."

As I pulled away to head home, I couldn't help but wonder if Phil was the real deal. Nice guys like this didn't exist, did they? Dancing with him made me feel like Cinderella — the ugly girl who enchanted the prince for a short time. I also couldn't stop thinking about how familiar he looked —

like I always knew him. He was someone I saw in the tunnel when I died, just like I saw Dan. That made me think there was something really special with him and this situation, but I'd been hurt before and tried not to get my hopes up.

Saturday came.
No call.
I gave up.
Done with men.

Sunday came. Phil called just as he promised he would, but I'm sorry to say that he didn't impress me. He could hardly hold a conversation and didn't seem interested in talking. I later found out that his lack of phone interest was the result of being extra tired from a bachelor party the night before. He asked if we could hang out soon. I agreed, thinking I'd flatter him with just one date.

The next day, Phil picked me up to go to a budget movie and out for ice cream. When he first arrived, he tried to be nonchalant, but as I appeared at the door ready to go out, wearing a cute black skirt and a tight white blouse with some black clogs, he looked me over from head to toe, making it apparent that maybe he had too much to drink when we first met and hadn't remembered what I looked like. But the smile plastered to his face that lit up the room suggested he was pleased with his choice. That made my heart happy.

On our second date, we had a sports competition, playing basketball and tennis — my two favorite sports that I played competitively most of my life. Going back and forth on both courts could be comparable to the couple in *The Cutting Edge* movie where the two ice skaters could hardly admit they loved each other as they competed. We fought like kids over whether the ball was in or out. He became frustrated with a hurt ego when I beat him in a shooting game of HORSE.

After losing, Phil responded, "I'm going to keep dating you until I beat you. No girl has ever beaten me before, and you know I'm a decent athlete as I played college baseball for four years and I even started too."

"Well, looks like you'll be dating me forever then." I confidently rubbed the win in his face. I thought it was cute that he wanted to impress me with his past status of being a college baseball player. I laughed thinking how different baseball is from basketball.

Being overly confident, naive, and perhaps a little stupid, I said later as we ate our Oreo custard treat, "I think you and I will get married someday." Phil's eyes enlarged like a frog's and looked as if they popped out of his head. Understandably so. Mine would have too. The shock on his face looked as if he wanted to run for the border. For whatever reason, though, he didn't run. Instead, he became intrigued with my boldness.

I know it's not the smartest idea to tell someone that you think they are "the one" on the second date, but I knew things would work out. I already saw Phil as an important part of my future when God showed me a glimpse of him years ago. God couldn't be wrong. But, I forgot that not everyone has that intuition developed like I do. Phil laughed and almost choked on his food, saying, "You don't know that I'm the heartbreaker. I'll keep ya around just to prove you wrong and break up with you," he said with a smirk and confident tone.

"Okay, we'll see …" I said back jokingly.

Chapter 6: Bible Verses on License Plates

Ask and it will be given to you. Seek and you will find; knock and the door will be opened to you. For everyone who asks receives; those who seek find; and to those who knock, the door will be opened.

— Matthew 7:7-8

Even though I moved to Illinois to teach at a new school, Phil and I maintained a long-distance relationship for over a year. Phil finally said that if I could find a job in Wisconsin near him, we'd get engaged. While he loved visiting me in the Chicago suburbs, the horrific traffic proved unbearable and tested his patience and ability to keep road rage at bay. A drive that should take only five or ten minutes could take over forty minutes in the Chicago suburb where I lived. With his encouragement, I eagerly applied everywhere, feeling a bit desperate. At this time in 2002, teaching jobs were hard to come by with most jobs having four hundred applicants per job opening. When a job opened up in the same Milwaukee suburban town where Phil lived, I couldn't wait to apply. I even wrote in my cover letter to the administration that if they believed in love, to give me the job, so I could marry my sweetheart and live in that same town. Turned out they did believe in love or maybe my teaching ability because they offered me a job teaching AP Literature, which happened to be my specialty. The opportunity felt meant to be, and the timing was perfect.

Meanwhile, Phil's best friend BJ continued to hound Phil to go out with him all the time — to the bars, to play cards, to ball games. BJ liked to hang with the guys a lot. At that time, Phil and I didn't realize that his best friend felt a loss of friendship, and as a result, started to cling to Phil and act jealous of our relationship. Because Phil chose to spend more time with me rather than with BJ, he falsely perceived that I controlled Phil's use of time and didn't understand why Phil chose to be with me rather than with the guys.

Nevertheless, BJ acted sincere when he congratulated us on our engagement giving us a nice bottle of wine and gladly accepting Phil's offer to be one of the groomsmen. I knew BJ for the past two years and considered him a friend as well. Phil and I believed BJ was sincerely happy for us.

After being engaged for almost two months, BJ offered to take Phil out to lunch, something that they did often. Unlike most lunch discussions about sports or work, BJ told Phil that they had to have a serious conversation about Phil's future. During their discussion, BJ said that "God talked to him" and, with a red face and a serious tone, said, "Phil, I'm sorry, but I can't support you marrying Christine."

"What?"

"I know. But I looked at a Bible verse this morning as a sign. Like what the verse describes, you haven't been yourself since you met Christine, and you no longer seem to have fun playing cards and drinking with the guys. You just don't seem happy. I don't think you guys should get married, and I'm going to have to step down from being a groomsman," BJ insisted.

Floored at what BJ just said, Phil listened to him, but felt like someone stabbed him, bursting his bubble of excitement over marrying the love of his life.

When Phil came home after lunch, he wouldn't talk or look at me. The tension that permeated throughout the room made me pace back and forth. "What's wrong?" I finally said, feeling concerned.

"It's nothing," Phil insisted.

"Um, something is bothering you. What is it? C'mon. Tell me."

"Well, I just don't know what to think. I love you and want to marry you, but my best friend just said he thinks you control me and that we are not good together. He feels so strongly that he decided to step down from being in our wedding. I'm just so confused. Maybe he sees something that I just can't see. I don't know what to think."

"What? Are you kidding me? How can he say that? He just gave us an engagement present. And how can you even doubt us?" I yelled in shock as tears started uncontrollably rolling down my cheeks.

"I don't know, but I need time to think. If my best friend says this, maybe he sees something I don't see. I need to figure this out and soon."

"This is crazy! What examples or explanation did he give? I don't get it. And, what's worse, how can you even believe him?"

Frustration engulfed my entire being. Phil's confusion and hesitation made me throw my engagement ring at him. I wanted him to be confident that I was "the one", and he wanted the same. BJ ruined our engagement and possibly our future together. Wanting to scream at the top of my lungs, I walked briskly to my bedroom where I cried into my pillow for hours until my red, puffy eyes could no longer take any more trauma.

Unfortunately, BJ's words cut deep and made Phil doubt the two years of fabulous times we had together. I reminisced about all the deep talks we had about life while hiking, fishing, and boating, our fun times with friends at music concerts and restaurants, our special times playing each other in sports like our lives depended on it, and attending ball games, our road trips, as well as all the times we celebrated together at our friends' weddings. The list went on and on. We fell in love quickly within a matter of weeks, and people claimed that we were that special cute couple that lit up when we were in each other's presence. After thinking about all our special times together and how I didn't want to live without Phil, I begged God to slap Phil across the head with a sign — to speak to him loudly and clearly to let him know that BJ's assessment of our future marriage was incorrect as he didn't really know me or us as a couple. His selfish meddling hurt me deeply, and as a result, I didn't know how to forgive him, especially if our marriage didn't happen. I felt betrayed — not just by our friend BJ — but by Phil too. The wound of betrayal could not be fixed with a simple Band-Aid. We needed help and immediate clarity. Without a doubt, we needed God to provide wisdom.

We didn't throw in the towel right away, but each day that went by while in this holding pattern of confusion and hurt felt like an eternity. A week after BJ's announcement to drop out of our wedding, Phil and I sought out a Christian marriage counselor. On our drive to see her, Phil and I cried on and off as it was the first time we were together that week. While stuck in traffic, we both saw a license plate that caught our attention. It read "Eph. 4:20-32".

"That's strange. Who would put a Bible verse on a license plate?" I asked while I pondered what it could mean.

"Write that down on the napkin in the glove compartment so that we can look it up after our appointment and see what the stranger thought was so important with that verse," Phil said urgently.

Five minutes later, we arrived at the counselor's office. I said a quick prayer that God would work through this lady to help save our future marriage. In the middle of the session, the counselor asked Phil, "How are you better since you met and fell in love with Christine?" With many complimentary answers saying that I was his best friend, that he loved hanging with me, that he could talk to me and tell me anything, that he never felt that way about anyone else, the counselor then had him compare what he was like before meeting me.

"Well, I'd play baseball, go out to the bars, play cards, and do guy stuff."

"So, are you a better person with Christine?"

"Well, yeah," Phil said, "but I want a sign. I need to know that Christine is the one. I'm looking for confirmation to know that this marriage to Christine is what God wants. When we first met, I had a feeling she was the one. I knew she was special right away — so much so that I knew I was supposed to marry her. Over time, I even got strange feeling that I was meant to inspire her to write a book. When I met her at the zoo the first time, it was like God told me she was 'the one'."

"Well, it sounds to me like your new self is better than your old self. There's some Bible verse in Ephesians about being your true self that you should look up later. I think it would help you. After hearing the dynamics of your friendship with BJ, I think this BJ is the one who is controlling, not Christine. Don't worry. God will give you a sign when you least expect it, and when he does, you will just know."

Hearing the counselor say what she did about BJ made me smile inside because someone else confirmed what I thought. Someone else saw the truth I saw, which gave me a tiny glimmer of hope that maybe Phil would come to his senses.

"Yeah, I hope it is sooner than later. We are supposed to get married in four months," Phil pleaded desperately. "I want this to work out," he added, "but don't want to go into it unless I'm 100 percent sure," Phil muttered sincerely and with a look of trepidation.

Back home, we looked at the Bible verse that was on the license plate when we drove to the counselor's office. The verse read, "You were taught with regard to your former way of life, to put off your old self, which is being corrupted by its deceitful desires to be made new in the attitude of your minds, and to put on the new self, created to be like God in true righteousness and holiness. Therefore, each of you must put off falsehood and speak truthfully to his neighbor, for we are all members of one body."

"No way! That's the same verse that BJ used at lunch when he tried to convince me not to marry you, but he took it out of context, and it's the same one that the counselor referenced us looking up tonight. Unreal," Phil said in a hopeful voice.

I couldn't believe it. We automatically cried reading this passage and hugged each other tightly as we knew it was our sign from God that we desperately needed and asked for. Neither of us could debate that God talked to us loudly and clearly through His biblical word. The counselor just pointed out how Phil's new self with me was better than his "old self" with BJ and the guys. I thought about how BJ must have been misled as he did not realize that Phil became a Godlier man with me than he ever was before. The new Godly Phil encompassed who he truly was and who he was meant to be.

The rest of the Bible passage read, "In your anger, do not sin. Do not let the sun go down while you are angry and do not give the devil a foothold. He who has been stealing must steal no longer, but must work, doing something useful with his own hands that he may have something to share with those in need … Get rid of all bitterness, rage, and anger, brawling and slander, along with every form of malice. Be kind and compassionate to one another, forgiving each other just as in Christ God forgave you."

Amazingly, this verse provided the outline of how we were to act toward BJ in a difficult and hurtful situation. We had to forgive him — no easy task for almost breaking up our future marriage. In the end, the struggle blessed us as it brought Phil and me closer and made us know we "were meant to be" as we both already knew in our hearts. BJ did not get his way in breaking up our marriage — four months later, we married as planned and still are happily married decades later. As for BJ, he whined to other friends that they should not go to our wedding and tried to convince people that they should talk Phil out of it before it was too late. Most friends ignored BJ's commands. But those who didn't, came back years later after BJ went through two of his own divorces, saying how sorry they were for listening to him. Over the years, BJ lost many of his friends while Phil found his.

Chapter 7: Angels and Signs from Above

Death ends a life, not a relationship.
                    —*Mitch Albom, Tuesdays with Morrie*

While weddings usually bring joyous times, they also
sometimes cause people to reflect on their loved ones who
could not be with them on their special day. Two of the people
whom I loved most — Smiley Dan and Grandma — would
sadly not be at my wedding.

As a little girl, Grandma always called me her "little
ladybug." Whenever I saw one, she said I should think of her,
and I'd have good luck. She wanted nothing more than to dance
at my wedding. While I waited anxiously in the church waiting
room, my maid of honor, Amy, brought me a card from Phil.
Inside, he wrote me a special love note with a bunch of ladybug
stickers to remind me that Grandma was still with us in spirit.
Crying and trying to not ruin my makeup, I proceeded to walk
down the aisle, ready to see the love of my life. Just as I
stepped on the runner to walk down the aisle, a little red
ladybug landed on my dress. I smiled and knew in my heart that
this had to be a purposeful encounter and not a coincidence.
Somehow, an angel provided reassurance through an obvious
sign that I would know that she was with me in spirit for my
special day.

As the bridal processional started, a large roar of what
sounded like thunder came out of nowhere. Oh great, I
thought. It's going to rain again. I couldn't help but worry
about how pictures outside would not happen. But then, as the
thundering roar of many engines continued, it became obvious
that a parade of harmonious motorcycles whizzing by created
the disturbance. I felt like they saluted my special day. As I
stood, looking at my handsome, soon-to-be husband Phil, the
motorcycles made me think of Smiley Dan. He certainly
always had a thing about timing — usually coming to
important events at the very last minute. Smiling, I knew that
the people we love most never really die. Love never
dies. God says in Psalm 91:11, "For he will command his
angels concerning you to guard you in all your ways." God

gave me a special gift on my wedding day: very specific signs that Dan and Grandma were both there.

PART III: Unanswered Prayers

If we look to nature, we see how there is a natural cause and effect, and for every action, an equal and opposite reaction. Comparing that natural law to our lives, we can see how nothing is random — including the chaotic storms in our lives. When our lives are most out of our control, we become receptive to the guidance that we wouldn't have had before. In the Bible, Job had to accept all that God asked. He was not owed or really given any explanation for God's decisions. The story of Job focuses on questions about God's justice and why good people suffer. It also shows that while we don't know why we suffer, we can bring our pain and grief to God and trust that He is wise and knows what He is doing.

Everyone at some point will have a season where life's waves crash down so hard that you start to drown in sorrow, wondering if you will make it out alive. Unfortunately, friends, it's certain that we won't escape this life without difficult times. Your storm might be the loss of a job or loved one. Perhaps it is a life-altering health diagnosis for you or a family member, or it might be the betrayal from a friend or a lover. For me, I struggled with years of infertility. In these dark and desperate times, people often turn to God for comfort. They pray and ask others to do so as well. Sometimes God answers these prayers right away. Other times, however, He is silent, and we must patiently wait until He is ready to show us the path. Our relationship with God is not like driving up at a fast-food restaurant and ordering what we want. However, I tried to do just that by seeking advice elsewhere. That silence can feel beyond lonely, making you want to take control of your own destiny. In the years of my yearning for a family, you will see how God gave me the free choice to try and answer my own prayers, but in doing so, I followed false prophets and went down a path that caused me tremendous pain.

Chapter 8: God's Silence-Unanswered Prayers

Character cannot be developed in ease and quiet. Only through experiences of trial and suffering can the soul be strengthened, vision cleared, ambition inspired, and success achieved.
— Helen Keller

I wanted to be a mom more than anything. Phil and I often imagined what our future children would look like. Would they have blonde, wavy hair and hazel-blue eyes like their mom or dark, thick hair and blue eyes like their dad? Either way, we both agreed they'd be cute! We wondered if they'd be athletic and enjoy playing sports like we both do or whether they'd have musical or artistic ability. Would they enjoy reading and writing like Mom or politics, business, and science like Dad? Of course, we both agreed that whatever their God-given talents were, we would do our best to raise them as kind, Christian children and not try and make them out to be just like us. We pictured how fun it would be to take them to various zoos, parks, and family vacations. We would often go into stores and play with the toys we wanted our children to have someday. Dreaming of going to Sesame Place or Disney World thrilled us both and tugged on our heart strings, making us wish we were parents already. This strong yearning for a child appeared only after a month of trying.

After the second month of trying, I felt fatigued and bloated. Not only that, I had to run to make it to the bathroom, and it seemed I had to go every hour. I felt little sparks of shooting sensations in my abdominal area. It must be an embryo implanting, and with all my heart, I knew that I had to be pregnant. This was it! I never had symptoms like that before, and I prided myself in knowing my body well. I had almost every symptom of pregnancy that I Googled and that my friends told me to look for. Slowly, I took out my first pregnancy test, praying and hoping it was positive. *Please, God, let this be it!* I broke out into a sweat with nervous anticipation. My heartbeat raced a mile a minute as I peed onto the stick. And there it was. One pink line. But where was the other one? One line meant "not pregnant". Thinking there was an error, I did another test. One pink line again. What the heck? Was I crazy? What did all my symptoms mean? These symptoms were more exaggerated than a normal period. Things felt different.

"The symptoms of getting your period can be much like feeling pregnant at first," nurse Jenny said when I called the OB/GYN's office to discuss. "Just keep trying every other day after you get your period. I'm sure we'll be hearing that you're pregnant before you know it. You're young yet, and it often takes many people a full year to get pregnant, even when nothing is wrong. Don't forget that, and try not to worry!"

I hung up, feeling that something just wasn't right. I had no reason to believe I was going to have fertility trouble, but for some reason, I just didn't think it would be an easy road. Each month around the time I should get my period, I felt pregnant with the same symptoms as the month before, but only one line appeared each time I tested. I was dumbfounded and in disbelief each time. The negative home pregnancy tests made me feel my mind played tricks on me, making me crazy.

Christian friends and acquaintances did not help either. They gave me all the clichés: "Just trust God," or "You're not trusting enough." And my all-time favorite: "Maybe you did something wrong and aren't deserving." Crazier yet, more than one person asked me, "Did you think about making sure you keep your legs up after you have sex?" I became so stressed out from the process of trying and from the pressure I'd feel after people's stupid comments. I often heard, "Maybe you are not relaxed enough. Just drink some wine and relax. Go on vacation again." I wanted to throw up and scream each time people tried to fix me and solve my infertility. They had no clue but to suggest that I didn't trust God enough or that I did something to deserve my fertility struggle. Who were they to act as though they were better people because God blessed them with kids?

Between my eighth and ninth month of trying, I skipped my period. Beyond excited that it must mean I was finally pregnant, I took a test. Another single pink line. Tears poured out like a dam broke. How could this be again? It didn't make sense. It had only been nine months of trying, but early on, my gut said I would have trouble in the baby-making department. I already saw one of the best fertility acupuncturists, but it was hard to understand Dr. J as he could barely speak English, so whatever he said with his thick accent sounded pretty good to me. I told myself I had to trust his work and the process. "It's just a matter of balancing your spleen with your liver and heart. There's nothing really wrong with you; just a slight hormonal imbalance." But, as the weeks turned into months, and the special Chinese herb concoctions, which involved lots of little black pellets, did not work, I decided that wasting $70 three times a week wasn't for me.

After skipping my period and around the time I should have gotten my period again, I started to feel cramping that felt like knives stabbing me. At times, it felt like something punched me from inside my belly. My lower back ached, making it difficult to walk, and I felt I could pass out any minute. Then, as I felt something pour out of me, I rushed with alarm to the bathroom to see a large circular two by two-inch blood clot in the toilet. The blood continued to pour out quickly, not stopping. Full of fear, I wondered if the acupuncturist messed my hormones up? What was going on? I couldn't be pregnant. The home pregnancy test was negative. Immediately, I frantically made an appointment to see my OB/GYN a few hours later. In between calling the OB/GYN and waiting for my appointment, I texted about my alarming blood clots and concerns to my best friend who was a critical care nurse. Amy texted back immediately, saying, "You could be having a miscarriage. I'm glad you are going to the doctor."

"How? There was only one line on the home pregnancy test."

"Yes, but the home tests are not as sensitive as a blood test that you'd get in a lab. You need to register at least 50 HCG (pregnancy hormone). You might have been pregnant but had less hormone to detect if it was early."

"Wow. I never thought of that. Got to go. I'm at the doctor's office," I texted back.

Worried and beyond afraid, I laid on the sterile exam table as blood continued to pour out. The doctor pulled out an embryo, and with no emotion, put it in a jar. "I'm sorry, but you've suffered a miscarriage. We will send it off for testing, as well as take your blood to see how much HCG pregnancy hormone you have. We will need to monitor you to make sure the HCG goes back down to zero."

"What? A miscarriage? How is that possible? I took a

test when I missed my period!" I said confused. Even though I knew theoretically from my best friend's thoughts that a miscarriage was a possibility, I still couldn't believe it could be true.

"You must have taken the test too early. It must be further along sometimes for it to show up on those at home pregnancy tests. Don't worry. Many women suffer miscarriages. It's common. You were saved from a baby that could have been abnormal, and you wouldn't want that. And you weren't very far along anyway, so you can try again soon. If it shows on the lab test that you were really early and your HCG is not too high, I don't think you will need a D & C (dilation and curettage to clear the uterine lining after a miscarriage)."

I couldn't believe what she just said and that my best friend was dead on. How insensitive! At that point, I resigned myself to fire her and never come back to this doctor or place again. I didn't care how common miscarriages were. That fact didn't take away that I wanted this baby as well as a successful outcome. Devastated, before leaving the exam room, I looked at the little embryo in the jar and sobbed as I said goodbye to what could have been. In sharing the sad news with Phil, he tried to cheer me up, saying, "Well, we at least know you can get pregnant now. It's just a matter of time. Don't worry, hun, it will be okay. Maybe this is a good sign."

I wanted to believe Phil that was right, but from the moment Phil and I started trying for a family in 2005, I often felt like Job because my faith was constantly tested. The longer my prayers for a child went unanswered, the more I felt unloved, frustrated, and even furious with God. I waited, and waited, and waited some more. I didn't clearly see until looking back how God carried me through these challenging times. He tried to throw me a life preserver, yet because I wanted answers that God did not give me, I went elsewhere for them. As a result, I could not see or hear Him correctly.

Phil, on the other hand, had faith like a child. He trusted God and the process and felt it was just a matter of time before we became parents. Phil often said that we had to enjoy our peace and quiet while we could. We saw our friends who had to get babysitters just to go out to dinner and who lost all their freedom and time to themselves. "Please enjoy what we have now, Christine. Someday, we will wish we could have this time to ourselves."

"But I don't care. I want to be a mom now. I'm so scared that it will just be us for the rest of our lives. No offense, hun. I've just always pictured us being parents. A childless life is not what I signed up for," I tried to explain, but it felt that he could not put himself in my shoes no matter how much he tried. I couldn't find that inner peace of mind that he had, and I felt jealous of his faith when doubt consumed me. Even with the doubt, I couldn't wait to try again. I had a goal, and that's all I focused on. Focusing on the future allowed me to falsely ignore the present pain for the time being.

When given the okay to try again, I had another miscarriage, and another and then another. Yep. I totaled well over thirty chemical pregnancies that ended in miscarriage in a period of seven years. Yes, you read that right — over thirty, and for sanity purposes, I stopped counting after that. A chemical pregnancy is a conception "which has measurable HCG but does not develop far enough to be seen on an ultrasound." In other words, the only evidence that an early pregnancy existed is the measurement of the HCG in a woman's blood or urine in a lab setting.

After the second miscarriage, I went back to Western medicine. The first reproductive specialist said after many tests, "I expect you to get pregnant within the year as nothing is wrong with either you or your husband." I didn't believe him. Surely, the fact that I was getting pregnant and having early miscarriages meant something was really wrong. Duh! Wanting control, I went to a new OB/GYN. Dr. Smith suggested I try fertility drugs. "I don't really know if you need it as you ovulate well already, but they often work, and we don't know why. Why don't we try three cycles with Clomid? Clomid is an infertility drug that is used to stimulate ovulation. Your only risk is that you might have twins."

We don't know why? Ugh. I came for answers, and she's just guessing at what to do. So annoyed, I just wanted to know what was wrong with me. Why couldn't the doctors figure this out? Wasn't that their job? I didn't want to take some random fertility drugs. I also felt completely helpless and that I had no other choice. I was stuck. Feeling desperate for something proactive to do, I decided to try the Clomid at the lowest dose possible.

Weeks later, I felt what a 50-year-old woman going

through menopause might go through. The hot flashes scared me. Waves of heat overcame me out of nowhere, leaving me dripping in sweat. I hated every second of it. My eyes twitched randomly. I am sure some of my more arrogant students thought that I was in a funny mood by winking at them. The final straw, though, occurred when I fainted and tripped coming up the stairs at work. I must have looked like a crazy woman.

I immediately called Dr. Smith. She said that those drugs never created symptoms like that, so that I must have something neurologically wrong and advised I go to a neurologist ASAP. In a ten-minute appointment with the neurologist, he conveyed with confidence that my side effects were the evil doing from the fertility drugs.

Why, God? Why? I questioned as I left the office. *Why must I always be in the one percent where I have the weird side effects with any medication I try? Oh, please just let me get pregnant and be done with this craziness.* But God didn't answer, and His silence felt like betrayal. To relax and get my mind off everything, I looked for a stack of business cards in my desk drawer, hoping I had one with a special deal going on. And there it was — a business card from Beth, a massage therapist whom I met years ago at a yoga class. That's just what I needed — so I thought.

It was the summer of 2006, and as I lay restless on the massage table, Beth said confidently, "You will ovulate on your right side, and your ovaries don't like the Clomid. Your body says you should stop right away."

What the heck? My body talks to her? How can she know this? I thought yet kept listening to her every word.

"You have blood clots stuck from past miscarriages. You should have had a D & C, but your doctors screwed up. I can energetically release these clots for you. Also, your body is tired of getting pregnant and of losing the embryos all the time. You conceive almost every time you try, but you lose your precious, perfect embryo, during the implantation process."

Really? Did I hear her correctly? Finally, someone verified that I conceived every time. Thus, my pregnancy symptoms weren't all in my head. Beth helped provide me with much-needed answers. Since my first two miscarriages, I knew what being pregnant felt like, but for some reason, the pregnancies were no longer showing up on the home pregnancy tests as the HCG was too low to detect. In hindsight, we knew they wouldn't show up as I lost these pregnancies in the late implantation process and the pregnancy hormone (HCG) was not at 50 or above to detect the pregnancy.

After Beth's session, I started cramping and bleeding a lot, so much that it made me hunch over in pain, bringing me to tears. Since it was only during the middle of my cycle, this bleeding was abnormal for me. Beth said it was all the past clots releasing, which was what was needed. I completely trusted what Beth said since I now had physical evidence of Beth's words and work. Ecstatic that I felt God led me to Beth, I believed she would be the one to solve this huge fertility mystery.

With any fertility question or anything going on with my body, for that matter, I turned to Beth. She always had an answer. Those answers made me feel confident and in control again, especially when I felt impatient for answers and solutions. I liked that I took action on my goal rather than waiting on God to answer my prayer. With each cycle, I felt that pregnancy was on the horizon, and when a cycle did not work, Beth provided an answer that made sense — answers were what I needed for my sanity. Sometimes a cycle didn't work because I ovulated too early or too late or an embryo needed a better spot to implant, or I needed to take a certain vitamin/herb, or I needed to let go of anger, or my aunt or grandpa had to die first. Knowing the possible reasons for pregnancy failure each month made me feel like my ship would soon come to shore to dock after having been caught in a never-ending storm.

After a few months of working with Beth, she sent me to Cindy, a naturopath, who she felt could provide some natural remedies to balance my hormones. At my first appointment with Cindy in the fall of 2006, she looked at my chart and confidently said, "My record of helping people get pregnant is very good. I'm almost at 100 percent except for one client who was anorexic. Can't help someone if she's not going to eat. I'm sure your past parathyroid surgery did a number on your hormones. The fact that you have had allergies makes me think that you have too much yeast in your body, which we must get rid of. Also, if we just add some progesterone, I think that will stop you from miscarrying." So, each month, I sought Cindy's advice. She'd tweak the amount of this or that and act confident that the next cycle would "be the one". Even Beth basically guaranteed that I'd be pregnant by Christmas.

Christmas 2006 came and went, and devastation hit me like a storm. How could Beth be wrong? I didn't get it. And if she was wrong now, was she wrong in the past? I wondered how I knew what she said before was true? Just as I was about to say goodbye to Beth forever, she said, "Christine, it was supposed to work by December 2006, but sometimes things change with our bodies. There's something more to figure out yet. I want you to call this energy healer in New Mexico named Mike. He can help provide some answers for you."

After Beth said that, on my drive home, I asked God for a sign. Of course, the song "Listen to Your Heart" came on the radio. Wow. Unbelievable. I told God how I tried to listen to my heart. My heart wanted more than anything to have a baby. Why did this song come on now? What did it mean? Did it mean I should trust Beth's words and now turn to Mike too for help? I broke down crying at the steering wheel while at a red light. God said nothing. I needed him to talk. Nothing. No words. Just silence. Lost again, I searched for answers, and when I arrived home, I checked out Mike's website, thinking that this guy who lived in New Mexico could help me find the missing link to my infertility nightmare. I fully believed that God could talk through others, so maybe turning to Mike for answers was how I was supposed to listen to my heart — I confidently thought that then anyway.

Phil continued to pray that we'd be parents soon and remained faithful that it would happen in God's perfect timing. He thought my listening to Beth and Cindy and now adding Mike to the mix was a unique and crazy path, but he let me go down it anyway. He often referred to them as whack jobs and asked, "Why do you need a middleman? If God wants to talk to you or intervene, he will." That actually made sense to me but frustrated me at the same time because I felt exhausted waiting on God to bless us with a child. I hated God's silence. Because there were no guarantees that we'd ever be blessed with a child, I felt I had to keep actively doing things that made me feel in control and that made me feel I was solving the infertility mystery. In the past, if I worked hard at goals in my schooling or in my work life, I achieved it. It was that simple.

Working hard equaled achievement. I couldn't figure out what I was doing wrong in this baby-making journey, so I kept pressing on, believing that all my efforts would eventually produce positive results with a healthy baby.

Chapter 9: Answers in All the Wrong Places-False Prophets

If any of you lacks wisdom, you should ask God, who gives
generously to all without finding fault, and it will be given to you.
                                                            — James 1:5

My first session with Mike, the energy healer, happened over the phone as he lived across the country. I was quite skeptical at first; he explained how he could use Qigong to connect with a person's vibrational energy. Okay, fine. I supposed that could happen. Since our bodies are composed of energetic vibrations, he could manipulate vibrations to help heal someone. As he worked on me over the phone by tapping into my energy, he commented on how I had allergies and all sorts of anger in my heart from this journey. Duh. Anyone could conclude that someone with my record of miscarriages would carry anger, right? But he went on to say that I had some tightness in my pelvic area that could be creating implantation problems. It all made sense to me. In hindsight, his advice was very vague, and anyone could have come to that conclusion.

Wanting to believe in Mike's energy healing, I had several sessions over the next few weeks and months as I again felt better trying to solve my fertility questions by taking control of the situation. Hoping to have my precious baby, I became consumed in reading anything I could about energy healing and eventually volunteered to help Mike write his book on vibrational energy healing using a balloon. I know what you're thinking ... healing with a balloon — is she serious? But it was a desperate time. He taught me to meditate and to be with what is — looking back, that was maybe the only valuable teaching. In meditating along with praying, I could perhaps one day truly listen to my own heart, which would eventually lead me to find the right path.

In one meditation by myself, I felt a fun-loving spirit around me and had a conversation with it. It was more or less a daydream that felt very real. I saw a cute face of a baby. He looked just like the Gerber baby with a round face, puffy cute cheeks, and grey-blue eyes with long eye lashes. This spirit said, "My name is Noah. If you think about it, my name still meets your qualifications of a name: you have never taught a Noah, and it is two syllables to go well with your last name. But my name means more than that. Remember Noah's Ark?"

"Of course, I do."

"You must trust God, yet remain persistent and faithful. When you trust, I will be."

I couldn't believe it — a sign from God. I needed to trust God. I heard that before though. Unfortunately, I didn't quite get it. I continued to talk to both Mike, the energy healer, and Beth, the masseuse, and looked to them for answers; I falsely trusted that God talked to them better than directly talking to me. That didn't make much sense when I look at it now, but my trusting others' insights more than my own connection with God was all part of my journey. So from there on out, any time I'd get pregnant, we called the fetus "Noah," and I was sure that Noah would one day be born to me. I even went back to acupuncture to help speed up the process.

Those three grueling years of trying for a baby consumed my life on a 28-day cycle. During the first 14 days, I worried about timing sex perfectly to get my body ready to conceive. The last 14 days were filled with waiting and making sure I had enough progesterone and other supplement recipes to help promote implantation. And, then I almost had a panic attack each time it was the magic moment to take a pregnancy test, which usually said I was pregnant. After a positive pregnancy stick, I made an appointment with my OB. I tried not to get too excited with a result that most people would rejoice over because a few days later, like clockwork, I'd bleed blood clots, get depressed, and have to pick myself up again, analyze what might have gone wrong and repeat the cycle with hope that the next month would prove successful in making our dreams come true. The roller coaster cycle of pure torture both mentally and physically just never stopped. In addition, time didn't want to slow down for me — and with each birthday half-heartedly celebrated, by my mid-thirties, I started to lose hope with reminders that my egg quality would slowly dissipate as well.

Most of my friends had to walk on eggshells around me not to say or do the wrong thing. Obsessed with the goal of having a baby, I became an empty bottomless pit. Josh Groban's song, "Don't Give Up; You are Loved" became one of my theme songs. I would not give up, no matter how hard the journey became. Every once in a while, when the monthly death sentence appeared for my little embryo child, the song that I listened to in college with Smiley Dan would often come on: "I get knocked down, but I get up again. You are never gonna keep me down." Of course, Chumbawamba's song is about alcohol, but when I occasionally heard it during this rough season, I related it to my fertility journey and smiled that Dan seemed to give me a sign that he was with me — the people we love never really die. That love and connection lasts forever — a fact that provided me with comfort even after another monthly loss.

After one particular loss in February 2007, I went to Wal-Mart like I often did on Sundays. I handed my coupons to the checkout clerk, Gary, a man in his early 40's. "You'll have to remind me about your coupons, miss. I have short term memory loss from having three kids and from having my head cracked open in five places from a motorcycle accident years ago."

"Are you serious?" I replied.

"Oh yes. I was dead for 12 minutes. It's amazing what prayer can do."

"Do you really believe in the power of prayer?" I asked bitterly, thinking how my prayers had not been answered.

"Absolutely. My mom prayed for me the whole time. Heaven is great. It's so relaxing and loving. My life changed after my accident. I now get along with my mom; I met my wife, and I have three lovely kids."

I told him how he's lucky to have his life and his kids — how all I wanted was to have a healthy baby.

"Everything happens for a reason. Even your being in my line here tonight to hear how the power of prayer really works is not a coincidence. What's your name?" the man asked.

"Christine," I replied.

"Christine, I'll pray for you. God bless you."

At home that night, my mind kept replaying that encounter, which appeared to be purposeful. Meeting that man at Wal-Mart reinforced how I tried to pray continuously and not give up. I needed to trust God and His timing. I had been trying to trust, but sometimes it was easier to try and take control myself when I felt God's silence. I wanted God's timing to be mine. The overall journey toward parenthood was a marathon that never ended. In trying to have a baby, I ran, stuck forever on mile twenty-three with no end in sight. Dehydrated and exhausted, I kept quenching my thirst in all the wrong places. I wanted to quit, but whenever I thought that or thought I was crazy to keep going with failure in every direction, I'd get a new answer that made sense, or Noah would come to me in a dream. "Please don't quit. I will be your son someday." With that cute face that I saw in my dreams and with his persistent request, how could I stop trying?

While Mike and Beth continued to coach me and supposedly helped me heal my energetic past, I also went to a fertility support group. But rather than feel supported, I felt very lonely there as no one could relate to getting pregnant and miscarrying all the time. I hated that I couldn't find answers or find anyone to relate with. Loneliness was not just the feeling of being alone but also a wall of fear and depression trapping me in my endless maze of searching for answers. Janet Fitch's words on loneliness in her book *White Oleander* resonated with me:

> Loneliness is the human condition. Cultivate it. The way it tunnels into you allows your soul room to grow. Never expect to outgrow loneliness. Never hope to find people who will understand you, someone to fill that space. An intelligent, sensitive person is the exception, the very great exception. If you expect to find people who will understand you, you will grow murderous with disappointment. The best you'll ever do is to understand yourself, know what it is that you want, and not let the cattle stand in your way.

Were the cattle, all my energy healers, getting in my way? I knew what I wanted, and maybe I just needed to sit with that loneliness for a while and be okay with it. One lady at the support group said that her internist had some natural ways of helping to balance hormones, so I jumped on the answer quest again by becoming interested in getting to know this new doctor.

A week later I had an appointment with Dr. Kelly who was an internal MD and who believed in both western and eastern medicine. Dr. Kelly told me, "You need to regain your power back; you gave it all to Mike and Beth. You need to surrender to God and wait for his timing." In the meanwhile, Dr. Kelly wanted me to see a flower essence woman, Mary, to see if my "electrical system" was off. Dr. Kelly explained how a flower essence practitioner uses flower remedies to help others find emotional balance and wellness. Mary would give me vials of flowers ground into liquid that I was supposed to let sit so I could breathe them in the air much like a diffuser would do. Another energy healer? I wondered if I wouldn't be giving my so-called power away again. But I figured that if this doctor thought flower essences could help me, I'd better trust her advice. After all, I'm not a doctor. What did I know?

After getting about eight different flower essences, Mary said, "Your electrical system is off because of things in your past life. You have to heal and let go."

"What?" I hadn't considered past lives. My current life was enough to worry about.

"You had a pretty reckless past life. You drank and did drugs. Got raped and had an abortion and then killed yourself. You are a very old and wise soul, though, and have much to offer the world through your tribulations."

I seethed inside and didn't believe it. Who the heck was she to claim such ridiculous ideas? None of it felt right inside. My stomach gurgled like I had acid reflux and part of me wanted to throw up. However, a part of me felt powerless, wondering if this crazy story contained bits of truth. Well, isn't that great. I even had trouble in my past lives if there was such a thing. This absurd information put me over the cliff.

Needing answers again, I took this information to Mike and asked him to test it out. He came out with even more upsetting news. "The man who raped you is your current husband. That's why you are having trouble having a baby with him in this life. Also, the baby you killed was your best friend Dan."

"What?!" I didn't want to hear it. The fact that these energy healers said this, and I couldn't prove it one way or another, killed me inside — making me vulnerable and even more helpless than I was to begin with. These insane stories completely tore what was left of my heart; the remains scattered into thousands of pieces. Consequently, I started to feel irate with Phil for what he supposedly did to me in a past life that I didn't even know I believed in, much less knew was true.

"Why are you so short and irritable toward me all the time?" Phil asked. I cried as I shared these horrific tales with him.

Phil replied, "That's a bunch of garbage. You don't really believe that, do you?"

"I don't know what to think. All I know is that I hate these stories, made-up or not," I explained.

"You need to pray," Phil responded.

At a loss, that evening, I turned to my Bible and realized it had been awhile since I did so. Randomly, or maybe not so randomly, as everything appeared to happen for a reason, I turned to Jeremiah 17: 5-10.

The Lord said, "Cursed is the one who trusts in man, who depends on flesh for his strength and whose heart turns away from the Lord. He will be like a bush in the wastelands; he will not see prosperity when it comes. He will dwell in the parched places of the desert, in a salt land where no one lives. But blessed is the man who trusts in the Lord, whose confidence is with him. He will be like a tree planted by the water that sends out its roots by the stream. It does not fear when heat comes; its leaves are always green. It has no worries in a year of drought and never fails to bear fruit."

Unbelievable! God clearly spoke to me through this verse, yet I foolishly ignored him by continuing to believe that He worked through Mike, Beth, the flower lady, and Dr. Kelly. Through this verse, God advised me again to trust Him, not to depend on anyone else for strength. Blindly, while on the wrong path, thinking I trusted God, I realized later I hadn't been trusting Him because I relied on others and not on what God said TO ME!

After reading that, I turned to James 1: 2-8. Here, God said, "Consider it pure joy, my brothers, whenever you face trials of many kinds because you know that the testing of your faith develops perseverance. Perseverance must finish its work, so that you may be mature and complete, not lacking anything. If any of you lacks wisdom, he should ask God, who gives generously to all without finding fault, and it will be given to him. But when he asks, he must believe and not doubt because he who doubts is like a wave of the sea, blown and tossed like the wind. That man should not think he will receive anything from the Lord."

My eyes popped out shocked at what I read! This passage confirmed the entire lesson of my journey so far. I told myself I had

to persevere, to ask God for wisdom and to continue to
believe in Him. And then, after all that, I called Mike to work
on the book. Yep, I know, hard to believe I did that. I couldn't
help thinking how God must have disappointedly shook his
head at me like I was a confused and lost child, trying to find
her way home on the wrong road. Here, God just reminded me
to trust him, and I went and sought Mike's advice for more
answers, which I realized much later were not given by God.
Why did I do that? Many of the answers these energy healers
gave me were mostly correct, which caused me to become
addicted to working with them. I believed each answer
brought me closer to meeting Noah in real life. I didn't want
to give up on Mike's work because its mysterious nature
provided half-truths that both appealed and awe-inspired me.
There had to be something to his energy healing. But I started
to realize that when he said he received his ideas from
"spirit," that his spirit and my spirit were very different.

In early 2007, my husband came with me to New
Mexico to meet Mike and supported me in editing Mike's
book. Phil was not about to let me go to this crazy guy alone,
and he later told me that he prayed that I'd see the con artist
that he believed he was. While in New Mexico, I encountered
a different side of Mike that I never would have seen, had I
not met him in person. He walked around as if he were God
himself. When we relaxed at some nearby hot springs, he told
some strangers we just met how he was a gifted healer, artist,
and writer. He totally ignored me as I sat and listened. He
didn't make mention of how I was the writer and editor for his
book. I felt God whisper, "See, he's using you. You cannot
trust what he says to you."

When I came back to Wisconsin, Mike desperately
tried to hold onto me like a crack addict needing his dealer —
he wrote and called all the time, telling me not to give up and
that he would eventually figure out why my pregnancies
failed. As he told me this, "Listen to Your Heart" came on the
radio. No coincidence, I thought. I needed to stay true to what
I realized about this guy. He was a fraud. So were all those
energy healers who preyed on vulnerable people and profited
off them. The more I resisted him, the more he tried to
maintain our friendship by calling and emailing all hours of

the day. It felt like a tug of war between God and Satan. I wanted good to win, but at times, I fell and returned to letting him read my energy when I wanted answers about pregnancy. But then, as another false promise of a pregnancy occurred, I finally blocked all communication with Mike for good by the fall of 2007. Amen! I finally listened to God's nudges.

Chapter 10: Scripture Quoted When Least Expected

If anyone speaks, he should do it as one speaking the very words of God ... so that in all things God may be praised through Jesus Christ.
— 1 Peter 4:11

Nearly every year, Phil and I took what we'd call a "last vacation before we were really parents" trip. Since we continued not to have success in the baby-making department, we had lots of "last vacations." On one getaway, we went to Sarasota, Florida, where the rain ruined our beach plans for the day. We saw a flyer in our hotel that a spa was open next door. We called, and they just happened to have two cancellations made an hour before for the massage that we both desperately wanted. We were in luck as relaxation called our names.

While I prepared for my massage, Deb, the massage therapist, asked if there were any medical things she should know. I told her that I often had miscarriages and that there was always the possibility that I could be pregnant. She took the information in, and while massaging me, asked, "I know this is a personal question, but are you a Christian?"

"Yes. Why?"

"I'm sensing that God knows of your pain and your prayers for a child. Don't stop praying. If it is God's will for you to have children, you will. I don't know why I'm going to tell you this, but you need to read the book of Ecclesiastes."

"Why? What's it about?"

"I don't know. God just told me to tell you that. Sometimes God can speak through people."

Not another soothsayer with deceiving ideas, I thought, but Deb seemed different. She told me to read the Bible, and that I'd have to figure out why God wanted me to read that particular book. No energy healer before told me to do that. She then explained how she had several abortions when she was young, for which she had trouble forgiving herself. But later, she found God and through Him, she had been very blessed. Because of God, she was able to leave her career in business and pursue helping people through massage. As she told me that, I thought about how I left business to become a teacher, following the path God led me to. She went on to explain how she waited several years for God to bless her with just the right man, so she understood the pain of waiting on God. Wow! We wanted what each other had. I wanted her fertility blessings while she wanted love like I found with Phil.

Hearing of her difficulties and desire for a loving man made me reflect on how blessed I was being married to Phil. He was a good guy — always supportive, loyal, and loving, and most importantly, my best friend. It was a long time since I counted my blessings, and it was helpful to think about something in my life for once that was truly good. I was stuck in my own negative muck for so long. Perhaps being grateful for my blessings would help me bring joy back in my life. I did not know what joy felt like anymore as I drowned in quicksand for way too long. Deb interrupted my thoughts when she asked if we could exchange email addresses, so that we could stay in touch and pray for one another. "Can't hurt to have another person praying for you," Deb said. I left, thinking about the irony of someone who did not want kids and aborted them to be the person God sent to encourage me to read a particular Bible verse. Life was full of surprises.

When I returned to the hotel after meeting Deb, I zoomed right for the dresser drawer on the side of the bed where most hotels kept a Bible. I quickly paged through, looking for Ecclesiastes and wondering what God had to say to me. Nothing seemed to speak to me until I read chapter 3: "There's a right time for everything….a time for birth and another for death, a right time to plant and another to reap, a right time to kill and another to heal, a right time to destroy and another to construct, a right time to cry and another to laugh, a right time to lament and another to cheer … a right time to hold on and another time to let go." As the passage continued, it said that there was nothing better for a man than to enjoy his work because that was his lot. A little further down the page, it said in chapter 11:5, "Whoever watches the wind will not plant; whoever looks at the clouds will not reap. As you do not know the path of the wind, or how the body is formed in a mother's womb, so you cannot understand the work of God, the Maker of all things. Sow your seed in the morning, and at evening let not your hands be idle, for you do not know which will succeed, whether this or that, or whether both will do equally well." These passages hit me like a lightning bolt, as tears rolled down my cheeks. I quickly called Phil over to hear what

God said.

"Oh my. God is basically saying that there will be both good and bad times in life. That there are seasons of pain but also seasons of joy. I won't have my season of pain forever, but that's where I am today. Basically, get on with my life and enjoy it."

"That's right, Christine. You know this lesson from before, right?" said my supportive hubby.

"What do you mean?"

"Remember your best friend, Dan? Didn't his dying young make you realize the importance of living life to the fullest? To make the most of each day? We discussed that the day we met at the zoo."

"Yes, that's true. How could I forget?"

"It's easy to forget when we are in the middle of a storm," Phil reminded me. "This is why I keep saying that we must continue having fun as a couple. You often get mad at me saying that, but I know that by living in the present moment, we will eventually find our joy instead of focusing on the past losses. Without joy, we will be stuck and won't have strength. Without strength, it's easy to get knocked down by the things that don't go our way. Seems like Satan likes to come right in and make us bitter when we are focused on the negative."

I sat on the bed, digesting what Phil just said. As I wondered in awe of where all his wisdom came from, I shed a few tears.

"Why are you crying?"

"Just thinking about how I'm grateful to have you as my husband."

"Of course, you should be." Phil smiled. As he hugged me, he said, "In Hebrews 13:5, God tells us that he is always there, speaking to us. We just need to listen."

Through both Deb and Phil, I realized that God wanted me to be joyful even if I didn't understand why I couldn't have my one wish for a healthy baby. The same lesson continued to wash up on shore after each storm: I was to trust that God had a plan and that I had to learn to be okay with the chaos of the storm. Still stuck in the eye of the tornado — maybe even more than I ever had been — reading

God's words about how my pain was part of a season that wouldn't last forever gave me just the hope I needed to continue and calmed my irritable heart for the time being. Basically, I had hope and faith that sunlight would come again soon. I needed to cling to that hope. Deb became my new pen pal for the next two years. While I encouraged her journey to trust that she would find the right man of her dreams and witnessed her go through heartaches in love, she encouraged me to keep the faith in my journey to Noah.

Chapter 11: God's Silence

When you pass through the waters, I will be with you, and through the rivers, they shall not overwhelm you; when you walk through fire, you shall not be burned, and the flame will not consume you.
— Isaiah 43:2

I clung to God's words as they provided me with reassurance that I was on the right path, that hope existed, and that I wouldn't be in emotional hell forever, yet, somehow, I fell off the path again as I continued to have miscarriages. Furious with God at his silence regarding my prayer requests, I couldn't understand how He would place the desire for a baby in my heart without fulfilling it. I wondered how God could expect me to trust him when my prayers were consistently ignored. It became apparent that God did not answer all prayers because it was just not in his will for me to have a biological baby, but what I didn't understand was why God wouldn't take away my aching desire for a baby. Why did I constantly need that thorn stuck in my heart? Somehow, I had to learn to become comfortable with the lack of answers and the unknown journey that kept twisting and turning. I felt like Alice in *Alice in Wonderland* who had to fall pretty hard down a deep dark hole, but I wondered if I'd ever get to the wonderland.

Needing answers, I sought Beth again. Why I felt that she'd have answers after having been wrong before, I'll never know, but being in my vulnerable state, I carried a spark of hope that she could help me figure out why my pregnancies continued to fail. I rationalized that no one could be correct 100 percent of the time. Insisting that she was a Christian, I thought seeking her advice would be fine.

Phil didn't like it one bit. "She's a false prophet," he said time after time. I ignored his warning.

Since my hubby continued to question Beth's advice, I paged through the Bible and randomly came to Romans 8:28: "And we know that in all things God works for the good of those who love him, who have been called according to his purpose." Through all my pain, there must be good that would come from this. I just wished it didn't have to be so painful and lonely. I remembered a quote from F. Scott Fitzgerald that said, "the loneliest moment in someone's life is when they are watching their whole world fall apart, and all they can do is stare blankly." I felt like that and didn't know how to keep going on with all this nonsense in trying for a baby.

Shortly after reading that verse and dwelling in my loneliness, a stranger from church called; she read my connection card (these are cards that the church puts out in the pews at church so people can write prayer requests) regarding all my miscarriages and felt the Lord tell her to call me. In her prayer, she asked God to give me wisdom and strength as well as to keep the devil away from me. Her point to keep the devil away seemed odd, but I didn't question it. She just happened to call on a night where I started my period after thinking I was pregnant, so I definitely needed to be uplifted. How did she know? Maybe God used her to help me in my moment of mourning.

Months passed by slowly, and Beth continued to be wrong about many of my potential pregnancies. She said I'd be pregnant after my Aunt Margaret died and before Christmas. She then said after one miscarriage, "What on earth did you do in your past life? It seems you are being punished now for whatever you did before. Not sure we can correct your behavior from the past."

"What the hell?" I said in disbelief. "Now, you are blaming me for my infertility and miscarriages. How dare you!" I shouted loudly as I hung up.

Horrified that she'd turn my infertility around and put blame on me after another miscarriage, I immediately fired her. I realized that by clinging to her, I delayed my true destiny. This time, I vowed a silent prayer that I'd stay away from Beth for good. I couldn't continue that crazy roller coaster for even one more minute. The hardest thing, though, about my belief that everything happens for a reason was that I had to wait for the reason to come along. More waiting. I wondered if I could manage waiting again.

In retrospect, the prayer from the lady at church was spot on — I needed to keep the devil away. Evil spirits work through others too, which I realized the hard way after years of listening to false prophets. God allowed the storm of infertility in my life to serve a bigger purpose. I falsely assumed that God's silence meant he was not present; I was blinded by my overwhelming feelings of numbness and shame from all the failed pregnancies. Not until later

did I know God was with me all along and that I didn't need
to turn my eyes and ears for answers elsewhere.

Chapter 12: God Speaks Through a Movie

Relying on God has to start all over every day as if nothing has yet been done.

— C.S. Lewis

Months dragged on. No Mike. No Beth. Just my lonely self who waited for answers, especially as everyone around me drank the fertility juice. Most of my friends were now large in the belly with their second or third on the way. Why had God forgotten me? Why couldn't I be blessed? What did I do wrong? Meanwhile, well-meaning Christian friends offered advice as they told me to enjoy my time without kids because they thought they no longer had a life. The constant desire of wanting kids and seeking ways to get them was no picnic either, but they didn't get it. Why couldn't anyone understand that? On one cold, February weekend in 2008, while stuck in my sorrow, Phil and I decided to watch a movie.

"What about this one? Where did we get this?" Phil asked.

"Oh, we got that at church a long time ago."

"What's it about?"

"I don't know, but let's try it. It's called *Facing the Giants* and looks like a good football movie."

Phil's eyes lit up as he welcomed anything related to football.

We watched the movie, and at first glance, it looked like a movie about a losing football team with a coach who was downtrodden. The players didn't seem to believe in themselves until they turned to God and really started working hard, praying, and trusting. Meanwhile, the coach and his wife had been trying for four years to get pregnant. Seriously! What were the chances of this being the movie we'd pick to watch? But the family's attitude inspired us. During their challenges, they continued to say that they would remain faithful and trust God even if things did not go their way. In the end, the lady did get pregnant and gave thanks to God through everything in both the good and bad times. It served as a model for us of how to deal with the unknown and how to have faith in the process.

After watching that movie, I realized I needed God

more than ever. In just those two hours, I produced an affirmation that I wrote and put on my mirror to remember each day. God said the following to me as I watched that movie:

1. Give God glory in all things
2. Surrender my will for His
3. God loves us; Trust him
4. Don't quit
5. Live in the present moment.

It wasn't that simple, though, because life's storms continued to pour down relentlessly on us both, but I now had a plan on how to live life, so that I would not drown. By having a relationship with God, rather than relying on false healers, I would stay afloat. The tears I shed from that movie felt like years' worth of tears finally releasing from a clogged dam; I kept so much inside that when the dam finally burst, the years of anger, frustration, and pain flowed right out. For a moment in time, I felt calm, happy, and refreshed—a little like the old me whom I'd forgotten from many years ago. That glimpse was someone I missed and wanted to see more of.

Chapter 13: Let Down by God

If there were no night, we would not appreciate the day, nor could we see the stars and the vastness of the heavens. We must partake of the bitter with the sweet. There is a divine purpose in the adversities we encounter every day. They prepare, they purge, they purify, and they bless.

— *James E Faust*

Since the lessons from the movie, I started praying more intensely, asking God for wisdom and His will. Shortly after these prayers, I started having very vivid dreams. It was now spring of 2008, and the voice in the dream said I needed to go back to see a reproductive endocrinologist (RE) and ask to have the recurrent miscarriage blood test as they would find some antibodies that caused blood clots. I never thought of that before. When I woke up, I quickly wrote that down and did some research. Sure enough, there was an antibody called cardiolipin that could cause problems with implantation like I had been having. When I saw the RE a few weeks later, he did the blood test and, to his surprise, but not mine, he said I had cardiolipin antibodies and should have them retested to be sure it was not a "fluke." Six weeks later provided the same results.

"Most people with this antibody take Lovenox shots with baby aspirin, but I think there's more going on here. I think you must have something else wrong."

More waiting! I thought to myself with hopelessness. It's one thing to get confirmation that some antibody caused miscarriage, and now another thing to say there might be more wrong. After all I'd been through, really? I felt like we were back to square one in trying to figure out this never-ending puzzle. So, I did more research and found a reproductive immunologist in Chicago. Dr. Case did the tests all over again and found even more antibodies. I appreciated the answers, even though I hated the findings.

"You need IVIG — basically antibodies to combat your antibodies. We will give you a three- hour injection of them, and they have a life of 28 days. Then if you're pregnant, we'll give you more." At $4,000 an injection, this better work, I thought. Beyond desperate again, I needed answers I couldn't provide, so I unfortunately turned to Beth after just having fired her. Reader, I know what you're thinking: why on earth would I go back to her after she was wrong so many times before and after she blamed me and my "past lives" for my miscarriages? The truth is that I couldn't handle her being wrong. I wanted her to be right because if she was wrong, it meant I wasted so much time and money working with her; I didn't want to be proven a fool for doing so. I rationalized, too, that she was right more than fifty percent of the time and that no human could be correct one hundred percent of the time. Like an addict needing her dealer, my addiction was in trying to find answers and solutions. I needed Beth to confirm the issue, and since I had been praying for wisdom, I thought this diagnosis was my needle in the haystack. Finally! After another appointment, Beth confirmed by looking at the energy in my body that the foreign antibodies caused most of my fertility issues.

I hoped for the best, but one night in my dream, I felt like something tingled and punched my abdomen. Then I saw Noah's cute and chubby face. "I'm sorry, but it's not going to work this time. Keep trying. I'll be back." Tears woke me up. I knew I'd have a miscarriage again. And like every other month, the Lovenox shots, the baby aspirin, and the IVIG antibodies produced the same result — an early miscarriage. Noah was right. Baffled and confused more than ever, I despised my life and everyone around me. Everywhere else I looked, I saw pregnant people. When one lady said it was an accident and that she didn't desire a child, I felt as if someone stabbed my heart. To take my mind off things and ease my pain, Phil took me out to dinner in some posh Milwaukee restaurant. In the bathroom stall, I noticed graffiti on the back of the door. Someone wrote, "if you think you can control your life, you're wrong. You must trust the guy upstairs. Trust me, it works."

"Oh, dear God. You're talking to me through someone's graffiti now and in a bathroom stall nonetheless?"

God replied, "Well, you need to know I'm still here and love you. I feel your pain and anger, and it is okay. I can take it."

I just couldn't believe it. I didn't know whether to laugh, cry, or scream. As I wanted to give up on God again, he reminded me how he was there for me in one of my darkest moments. He just wouldn't let go of me. He loved me even though I messed up and went back to Beth for answers instead of turning to Him.

Back in Dr. Case's office a few weeks later, she said that I should try IVF (in vitro fertilization) with IVIG to ensure that my egg quality was okay — not the step I wanted to do. IVF was the last resort — the big show and not to mention, at least $16,000-$20,000 with no real guarantee of a baby. If this didn't work, what would be next? I'd have no next move, a fact that worried me, making me hopeless and possibly broke.

I prayed non-stop about whether I should do IVF or not. The next day, on the radio while I drove to work, I heard a radio ad for IVF at the place in Illinois where I considered having it done. I switched the station and then heard "Listen to Your Heart". Of course, that song came on then. More confirmation, I thought, that that decision was the best and correct one. But what did my heart want? It just wanted a baby — that's all. Was that so much to ask? I wanted to meet Noah in person. It had been four years on my endless journey to nowhere. I continued to go around and around on my last leg of a marathon, but the problem was that the marathon never ended. I was tired. Tired of doctor's appointments, tired of hormone checks, tired of timing sex, tired of people giving unsolicited advice, tired of good-hearted people trying to fix me. Tired of it all. I wanted to quit, but I believed that Noah would be one day, and I believed I was only one answer away from that reality coming true. While I didn't really want to do IVF, I knew that I could not go forward if I hadn't tried everything in my power. I didn't want to look back with any "what ifs". So, a new roller coaster came my way, and once on it, I couldn't get off. This roller coaster went through a deep, dark tunnel with no light at the end.

Shortly after getting the news that I should consider doing IVF, I attended my husband's softball party where I saw a couple our age with newly born twins. Immediately upon seeing this couple, I wondered if their twins might not be natural. I hoped that this woman might have advice for me concerning good doctors for IVF. However, I couldn't just come out and ask her about it, so I struck up a conversation with her about her kids. I told her that we were trying and might have to consider IVF in the near future. Sharing my story opened up the floodgates of conversation. They had IVF twins — just as I thought. Even more ironic, though, was how she went to the same clinic that we considered using. Lisa did all the research, and as a result, had a wealth of information to share with us, which was great timing since we were too exhausted to do all that information-gathering ourselves. Looking back at this situation, meeting Lisa at that exact time seemed purposeful; God sent her to help me walk through the scary world of IVF, as well as to confirm that the clinic was my next step.

For weeks, we drove 1.5 hours to Illinois for injections, ultrasounds, mini-surgeries — all to make this precious little baby. Family members and friends across the country prayed for us. Every night, we practically begged God for this IVF cycle to work. After a rocky week of wondering if I'd have enough eggs and if they'd be mature enough to use, I was finally given the green light for the egg retrieval and then later the embryo transfer.

When we first saw the little picture of our two 8-cell embryos, I couldn't have been any happier or prouder. They were perfect. Even the doctor said, "These are great embryos. You have every reason to think that this should work." We knew that there were no guarantees, though. I kept reminding myself that we never did IVF before and that it felt as if God led us to do it. God would not let us down now, especially since I was so sure that we did exactly what God wanted us to do. And I had all the pregnancy symptoms one could ever ask for — that tingly feeling in my abdominal area, nausea, moodiness, fatigue, and frequent urination. Finally, the day of the blood test results arrived — November 8, 2008—do or die day.

"Congratulations," the nurse said. "You are pregnant, but your HCG is a little lower than normal. We'd like to see it over 50 at this point, and yours is at 39. It needs to double in the next 48 hours, so be cautiously optimistic. It still could happen," the nurse reported.

Ecstatic and naively confident, I thanked God and jumped up and down. God finally answered our prayers: pregnant after 3.5 years of continuously trying. We couldn't wait for these little embryos to develop, so that someday, I could hold them in person.

That night, Noah came again in my dreams saying, "I'm with you, but I don't think I'll be able to stay. I don't know why." These words literally woke me up at 3 a.m. I still had the tingling breasts, the urge to pee, the bloated feeling, no spotting — all good signs. I prayed that Noah was wrong and begged him to stay as I cried with worry.

Forty-eight hours later, the nurse called with the most recent blood test results. "I'm sorry, but your HCG did not double. It actually stayed the same."

"What? Are you sure you're not looking at the same results as two days ago?"

"I'm sure. We double-checked."

"So what does this mean?"

"Well, I hate to say it, but you will start miscarrying soon."

Noooooooo! No God! Please don't let this be true! My heart jumped out of my chest. In complete shock, I ached all over and felt as if someone stabbed me a thousand times. Minutes and hours seemed like days, weeks, and years. Like a robot, I mechanically spoke, moved, and did what programmed to do. No eating. No sleeping. No crying. I was comfortably numb as Pink Floyd sung — minus the comfortable part.

PART IV: Waiting and Trusting God in the Vortex of the Storm

After years of heartbreak and feeling that God did not love me, I hit an all-time low with numbness that made it challenging to even hear God's whispers. God knew this. As a result, he worked through others — a random stranger with a poem, leaders at a church retreat, and my pastor. God never gave up on me. Don't ever underestimate the timing and meaning of what others might say to you. It might just be God speaking through them to comfort you and to wake you up and guide you toward your purposeful path.

Chapter 14: God Sends People to Help

I know now that we never get over great losses. We absorb them and
they carve us into different, often kinder creatures.
                                                    — Gail Caldwell

Where was God now? He ignored all our prayers and
left us childless again. How could He? I trusted Him!
Overwhelmed with emotion, I wrote God a letter in my
journal:

Dear God,

I don't understand you at all. I am trying to trust you and listen to
you, but it feels you are not here. Why do you let me continue to
suffer like this? If I'm not meant to have kids, please just take this
desire away. Why do you bless so many others with kids and even
those who don't want them, but not us? Have we not been faithful
enough? I feel as if you lead me to an answer, only to have it not pan
out. Why all these false leads? I feel like you are a prankster. I go
down this road and then this one and that one — all which seem to
give false hope and ultimately fail. What am I supposed to learn
from all this? I've been in emotional hell for much too long.

Please, oh please, bless us with a baby or give us a sign that we are
not supposed to be parents. I can't take much more. Phil went up
north to go hunting and took all our knives. He was afraid that I
might do something stupid. I won't lie. I thought about how this pain
is so unbearable that I don't find much point in living anymore. If I
can't have children, I'll feel like something's always missing. How
can I keep living when everywhere I look, there is some cute family
discussing their milestones — the first day of school pictures, the
birthday parties, the t-ball games, the graduation parties. You name
it — there will always be constant reminders of what I can't have. I
feel like such a failure because I can't do what most women can. No
matter how hard I try, I just can't stay pregnant. So God, I beg you
to change the desires of my heart or bless me by answering those
desires. Every day is a struggle. Please help me. I'm at my breaking

point. I can't go on.

Love,
Christine

If God spoke to me, numbness prevented me from hearing him. My own pity party consumed me, and I falsely believed that God was not present in my life. I couldn't see how God tried to talk to me, but Bill Hybels explained in his book, *Whispers,* that "God cannot be seen by spiritual eyes that are shut. God cannot be heard by spiritual ears that are plugged. And God cannot be followed by a heart that stubbornly stays hard." On one particular morning, though, late in November after Phil had time to talk to God during his hunting expeditions, he took charge of our situation, saying, "I think it's time we look at adoption. I really think this is what God wants us to do."

"I don't want to," I shouted stubbornly. How could Phil give up? "I really want our own biological child — one who looks like us and can inherit our gifts."

"I want that too, but I think God has something else planned. How do you feel about me at least getting books on it and learning about the process?"

I rolled my eyes in my own internal temper tantrum. I didn't desire to adopt — that was the last thing I wanted to try. Resistant and stubborn, I finally mumbled after a long pause, "Sure, I guess research won't hurt."

For the next few weeks, we read up on international vs. domestic adoption and the process quickly overwhelmed us. While I wasn't fully on board with going the adoption route, I wanted to get our names in with an agency so that option would be there if we were chosen and because I knew that the adoption process could take several years. Picking the right adoption agency seemed daunting. With so many agencies and with being a perfectionist, I did not want to pick the wrong one. We ended up interviewing several agencies and took time to learn the pros and cons of each type of adoption and of each agency. Over the course of a week, God sent people to us who adopted themselves, and as a result, wanted to give back by helping us.

A friend of ours gave our name and email to one of her church friends, Jena, who adopted two children from Columbia. Jena emailed me right away, offering to be a shoulder to cry on or a listening ear. As I considered the adoption process, she shared her story of how she too didn't want to adopt at first. Without hesitation, she shared her fears — what if the baby would be born with severe psychological issues? What if the baby was ugly? What if the baby never bonded with her? What if she didn't ever love this baby like her own? The list went on and on, but by her being so honest and touching some of my prideful fears, I realized many of my reservations were completely normal. Not being alone and having her to talk to was a heaven-sent timely and purposeful miracle.

In awe of how God used other people to give us necessary information, I realized that God gave us confirmation of the right answer by having the same answer appear through other people on multiple occasions. We had our pros and cons list narrowed down to three Wisconsin agencies, yet not one of the agencies felt right. I couldn't quite put my finger on it. Maybe it was for the simple fact that I wasn't over the IVF loss or the idea of having a biological child. Because I always worked hard and achieved whatever I set out to do, having a failing body that didn't allow me to do what most women did naturally made me bitter and numb. Grieving those losses would be a lifelong process of healing and my own personal thorn to bring me closer to God.

We asked everyone we knew to pray for us in our critical decision of which agency to use. We also asked friends of friends to find out what agency any of their friends used when adopting. In a nutshell, we networked. After not hearing from anyone for a long time, on one January day, three different friends, none of whom knew each other, emailed me, telling me the name of the adoption agency their friends used to adopt from — Adoption Angels from San Antonio, Texas, they all said. No way, I thought. What are the chances of that? I could not believe it again. Our sign — the one we waited an eternity for. Immediately, I Googled Adoption Angels and liked what I saw. Within the hour, I talked to the agency's director and asked for their information packet. A week later, I had the initial information filled out, which included getting medical records, writing a ten-page autobiography on each of our lives, and since Phil hated writing, I had to write his too. We needed to humble ourselves by getting three non-family members to write recommendation letters for us saying that we'd be great parents. To be honest, that part of the process completely annoyed me. When people get pregnant, they don't have to be interviewed and ask for letters of recommendation to become parents. Within the month, though, I put my feelings of injustice aside and completed my social work papers from Wisconsin and Texas.

I spent several weekends making our scrapbook of our lives for the future birthparents to pick us from, making sure each picture told just the right story. One page showed the rooms in our home, another our immediate family members, another different sports and hobbies we participated in, as well as different trips we took. During this time, I felt compelled to think of what a future nursery might look like and included a picture of that too. I envisioned a colorful jungle theme, something that would keep a baby alert and interested, and at the same time, work for either gender. When I'd go to different stores that carried baby items, I gave myself permission for the first time to think about what the nursery might look like. I never could find the artwork I wanted, so one day, I went to Michaels, a well-known craft store where I lived, bought my supplies and canvas and painted a bright and colorful animal picture filled with a panda, lion, elephant, ocean starfish etc. I smiled and felt joy for the first time as I painted this special gift for our future baby.

By March, 2009, we were done with our home study and ready to adopt a baby. And the crazy thing with adoption was that it literally could happen at a drop of a hat. That's what we hoped for, anyway. But the old familiar story of waiting on God began again.

Chapter 15: God Speaks Through Others

People are meant to live in an ongoing relationship with, speaking and being spoken to.
                                                    — *Dallas Willard*

I thought I understood how hard waiting on God could be throughout the infertility process, but the longer the adoption journey lingered, each day without a baby felt like decades. I wanted my baby yesterday already. After months of feeling on hold, some friends from church invited me to a religious retreat to hear a well-known Christian speaker. I really could not bear to give up a whole weekend to hear someone I never heard of and almost cancelled last minute. I did not know these ladies that well, and it was not my style to sit all day and night praying and singing — especially singing. God forgot to bless me in the singing department, so I didn't like to sing in public. However, since I already paid my money, my frugality won out, and I did not want to waste it. I went, hoping for the best but not expecting much.

At the opening session, I found myself quite interested when the main speaker talked about how all of us have a thorn, something that had or will hurt us, but that God would use to transform us. The pain would not be wasted. She then quoted 1 Thessalonians 5:16, "Be joyful always; pray continually; give thanks in all circumstances, for this is God's will for you in Christ Jesus." Lisa explained that no matter what pain we went through, we should not give up.

I heard her words but blocked them out as I thought that she hadn't gone through what I had. She didn't understand the pain of infertility, of miscarriage, or of the pain of waiting on an adoption.

"I understand waiting on the Lord," Lisa explained. "I was angry with God and hurt for over seven years as my husband and I tried to have a baby with no luck. Three of those years, I was in a deep depression and could hardly get out of bed. My husband pointed out how I was bitter and had to trust the Lord would use my pain for good. I had to trust that there would be a season of joy again. I had to learn to capture the joyful moments and appreciate the blessings I did have."

As I heard these words, lessons of the past flowed back. In my obsession in trying for a baby, I had forgotten. One of the most important lessons I learned after Dan's and Grandma's deaths was to appreciate every little moment because our time in this world is so brief. As anger, bitterness, and numbness engulfed me the past few years, I completely lost myself. Even if the simple joys of life were right in front of me, I did not see them. I couldn't.

Lisa had us kneel in order to listen to God as we prayed. I hadn't knelt for the Lord since my Catholic school days and had no idea what to expect. As I kneeled there waiting, a floodgate of tears poured out like water releasing from a dam. It was not just because my knees cracked and hurt. As my tears cleansed my soul, I clearly heard God speak through my heart. "You don't need to fear. Trust me. I have great plans for you. You need to allow yourself to feel joy and excitement in the adoption process. You are on the right path. Write about this, and don't let your pain be wasted. You will help others. Keep surrendering and praying. You should know by now that not everything in life has an explanation, but that you must keep the faith, especially when you don't understand."

God helped clear some of my grief, and surprisingly, I felt happy for the first time in years; a heavy weight lifted from my shoulders, similar to how watching that faith-based movie cleansed me years before. And then it dawned on me — God's right. Well, of course He is. He is God, but I couldn't believe how I lived out my master's degree thesis like Grandma suggested years ago. I wrote a book about how to ask different types of questions to challenge students to think about literature and life. Students came to learn that answers to life's difficult questions don't always exist and that sometimes we just had to be comfortable with not having answers.

For years, I lived in the chaos of a foggy storm by wanting answers, but not having any made me uncomfortable. Over time, I accepted the unknown, and I grew in character as a result. I wanted answers so badly so that I could have control, but in reality, God was the only one in control. I went everywhere, looking for answers — to Western doctors, psychologists, acupuncturists, massage therapists, energy healers, homeopathic healers, you name it, and wasted valuable years searching for answers that I believed would heal me. No one gave me a clear answer, which made me quite crazy at times, especially when some specialists disagreed with one another. I continued to believe that if I persevered long enough, an answer would be found, and I could not help wondering why I'd often dream of baby Noah. I still yearned to meet him.

In the past, if I worked hard at something, I succeeded. However, in the quest for an understanding of why we could not have a baby, it just wasn't God's will for us to know — at least not in this lifetime. Maybe someday in heaven, I'd understand, but for now, I had to trust that some good would come out of my pain and continual losses. Deep down, I had to trust and believe that somehow, I could be happy again, even if things didn't ever go my way.

People would often try to make me feel better, saying that "everything happens for a reason." While I believed that to an extent, I started to realize that particular cliché was an "emotional distraction." In his article, "Why Everything Does Not Happen for a Reason," John Pavlovitz said that things don't always happen purposefully because that "cheats us out of the full measure of our real time grief and outrage." I'd been focused on trying to find out all the whys of my suffering, instead of just admitting that maybe there was no why or reason to be found. It was important for me to acknowledge that this pain of waiting and that not knowing why I couldn't have a biological child just plain stunk. While it is true in Romans 8:28 that "we know that in all things God works for the good of those who love him, who have been called according to His purpose," that did not mean we would be exempt from anything unpleasant. This anguish served as a catalyst for my greatest learning and needing to rely on God who also wept with me through my pain. While all my suffering might not have happened for a reason, there was meaning in how I responded and grew from this experience. In retrospect, God used my suffering for good, but in going through those storms, I couldn't see clearly at that time, which is often the case for all of us.

Shortly after this very powerful discussion and reflection with God, I went to get a neck massage on my break between sessions at the retreat. After all that heavy emotional vomit, I needed to relax. While being massaged, the woman asked if my neck was so tight over stress with kids. I couldn't help but laugh a little. "No," I replied. "But it may be stress over the process of trying to have kids. We're now waiting on an adoption, and the wait has been kind of long, especially after four years of trying for a baby."

"Oh. I'm sorry. I totally understand. I've been really upset that we're having trouble in that department as well, and it's been two long years for us. I've had a few miscarriages too. I'd like to hear more about adoption, but I'm not sure where to go or how to start."

Unbelievable. This couldn't be a coincidence. As my massage therapist started pulling my hair, her own anger shined. At the end of the ten-minute session, I was lucky to walk away with any hair left. She seemed so depressed, and even though she pulled on my hair over her frustration in her own infertility journey, I wanted to help her with what God taught me.

"Even though this journey is very painful and frustrating, you must still try to live your life and let yourself feel joy. I know it's hard to do and to tell ya the truth, that's my downfall. I have trouble living in the moment and realizing the blessings in my life; I still have my amazing husband, family, friends, health, job. I hate the cliché that it could always be worse, but that saying is true and a cliché for a reason."

We exchanged email addresses, and I promised to send her some adoption information to help her out. Like a child who just learned an important lesson and wanted to proudly show it off to her parent, I told the main speaker Lisa what just happened.

"Praise God," she excitedly said. "God healed you, so you could then help someone else who was in pain. See how He works? Now, you must write about it and continue to help and heal others."

I knew God used people to help others, but I just didn't think it could happen so quickly. When I came home, I sent the adoption information to the lady who massaged my neck. Sadly, I never heard from her again and often wondered what happened in her journey, but I believe our meeting was purposeful and God's way of showing me how I could help others with what I learned through my own infertility struggles.

About an hour after my massage, my friend, Bobbie, introduced me to another speaker who shared my name.

"Bobbie shared with me that you've suffered miscarriages and infertility for years. I'm sooo sorry. I understand. I struggled for four years, but now have four beautiful children," Chrissy said.

"Oh, wow. Did you find the problem?" I asked with interest.

"Did you ever see Dr. Jane? I finally found out I had endometriosis and went to her to have it removed as she is one of the best in the nation and is right in Milwaukee, of all places."

"I don't think that's my issue," I confidently stated, but then as I thought about it more, I wasn't so sure. Why was I so confident in my first response? My periods and cramps had always been heavy, and that diagnosis was one that I always wondered about but dismissed since doctors basically said it would not be an issue even if I did have it.

"Oh, yes. Endometriosis can totally affect a woman's hormones and cause infertility and miscarriage. Maybe it's something you'd want to check out," Chrissy urged me. "Just remember that God can do anything. I never thought I'd have even one child, and now I have four blessings. I didn't even have my first child until my mid-thirties," she said as she beamed proudly.

Confused again, I put my hands up toward God. Why would I meet this woman now? I already said goodbye to the infertility path. I literally just mourned it by shedding an ocean of tears. Why now? Putting someone like this in my path made me think that I should check out this potential issue, but the only way to do so was through a laparoscopy — and that meant surgery.

I just became comfortable with the idea that I didn't have any answers. Why should I care now? Why was I thrown this curveball with another possible reason for my infertility that I'd need to investigate? Couldn't God see how exhausted I was, especially when in the middle of an adoption, which I decided to be excited about for the first time? The timing of another path to explore annoyed me and tore my heart apart. It just didn't seem to fit the path I was on.

Chapter 16: God Whispers Through License Plates Again

To hear God's voice, you must turn down the volume of the world.
— Anna Christian

I decided to tuck away this lady's story as food for thought. I had no idea why her path would cross mine at that time. As I drove home one night from work, I heard DJ Delilah on the radio. For those of you who are not familiar with Delilah, she was a radio DJ who had people request songs based on some sappy story in their lives. I'll never forget how this one woman requested a song that had meaning to her becoming a mother. She told the story of how she was infertile for many years, but then God spoke to her and told her to ask Him for the blessing of children. This same lady ended up having a laparoscopy for endometriosis, which then allowed her to have biological kids.

As I listened to this story, I knew again that the timing of hearing it couldn't be a coincidence, but I also didn't understand what I was to take away from the story. It became clear to me that birthing kids was not in the cards for me. I often cringed when I heard people having success with pregnancy after having gone through so many years of trying because stories like these made me feel alone and forgotten by God. Why weren't my prayers answered? Why theirs? What did I do wrong? I started to doubt God again and wondered if I'd ever have a baby either through myself or through adoption. I asked God for a sign — for anything. Desperate, I'd cry alone at night, asking God to take away my pain or to give me a sign that all would be okay. God's silence slowly made me want to give up.

Again, as the pain of each day without a child or answer ached, I finally heard God in my heart while in the car with Phil. "Look in front of you." And there it was — another license plate message to me. The last time I had a message from God on a license plate was that Bible verse that helped Phil and me figure out that we were meant to be together and that our engagement should continue as planned. Now, in front of me on a blue pickup truck, a license plate said "believe. Believe what? I questioned God inside my mind.

God clearly answered, "Believe in me and what I can do." I smiled, nodded okay and felt a peaceful wave wash over me.

It had been months since I did In Vitro Fertilization and all those crazy fertility drugs that went along with that process, but my monthly cycles were oddly very heavy and painful as well. In discussing these changes with my ob-gyn, she said the only thing left to do would be to have a laparoscopy to check for endometriosis. Ta-da. A light bulb went off in my mind. Perhaps the reason for meeting the woman who had four kids after having endometriosis surgery was because I was destined for the same outcome. When my doctor explained that insurance would cover the surgery on the diagnosis of heavy periods, I jumped at the opportunity.

"Sign me up. How soon can we do the surgery?" I impatiently demanded. While my doctor wanted to do the surgery to see if endo was present so that she could remove it and reduce my pain, my secret goal, of course, was to improve my chances of keeping a pregnancy. Finding endometriosis had to be the missing needle in the haystack.

Just a few weeks later in June of 2009, I had my laparoscopy, and just as I suspected, endometriosis was found and removed through a laser. Perhaps that's why I met Chrissy and then heard the story on the radio of the lady who also had endometriosis. For whatever reason, it appeared that I needed to find out that I had this horrible disease. In doing more research, I learned that estrogen from fertility drugs could help the endometriosis grow and spread like wildfire. Had I never done the IVF, I might not have experienced the pain I did, which in hindsight, helped my doctor diagnosis me with endometriosis in the first place. Funny how things worked.

Hopeful that this new diagnosis was the magic answer that I waited on for years, I expected and believed with all my heart that a pregnancy was right around the corner. However, as the months came and went, the same circular pattern appeared — the symptoms of pregnancy appeared with much anticipation and excitement, but with enough time, they always resulted in a bloody mess. Beyond annoyed, I grew frustrated and angry again and again. How could God do this to me? Why did I get the diagnosis, but no solution? I never wanted to go back on this roller coaster, but somehow I did, based on signs to do so. Not understanding

God, my crazy journey, or life in general, I prepared to give up. My heart cried in immense pain and my head ached, full of fog.

Chapter 17: God Carries Me Through Life's Storms

The Lord is close to the broken hearted and saves those who are crushed in spirit. Even though I walk through the darkest valley, I will fear no evil for you are with me.
— Psalm 23

October 2009, six months after surgery, I impatiently waited and waited and waited. Nothing. No luck. The only positive result from that surgery was a little less cramping each month and a shorter period. None of my pregnancies worked and even worse, there had been very little action in having any adoption match. For whatever reason, our adoption profile had not been looked at — not even once. What was wrong with us? Why couldn't we be blessed with kids one way or another? I forgot again how to feel the joy in my life and slipped into a new state of numbness, so much that I did not feel like living. Nothing soothed my frayed mind. The clarity of my mind was so far gone that suicide seemed like a rational option; it was only a matter of time before I figured out how I would do so. God felt like a distant friend who forgot and betrayed me. Complete silence. Without God's voice and wisdom to light my path, loneliness overcame me as I felt ghosted by God. What could be worse than that?

At the lowest point in our journey thus far, we went to Saturday night service at church. I figured it would be my last one. We had nothing better to do than go to church since all our friends were in survival mode, caring for their babies and toddlers. None of them could afford to go out or hire babysitters. Oh, how I would have loved to have traded places with them as they complained about not having a quiet moment alone or not having the "freedom" that Phil and I supposedly enjoyed.

Bitter at the world, I sulked in my seat at church as Pastor Tom spoke on trusting God's plans for our lives. What plan? I thought bitterly. In emotional jail without any hope of joy, I longed to break free from the chains that kept me down. Tears flooded my eyes as I tried to fight them, but they continued to seep out one by one and eventually flowed like a steady stream. Sad and pissed off, I felt that Pastor Tom's sermon didn't apply to me, and again, that made me feel alone. No plan for our lives existed — just the same crap over and over with no end in sight. It felt like Ground Hog's Day every day. I trusted God as much as I could and still no child to call our own came our way.

After the service and concerned about my well-being, Phil dragged me toward Pastor Tom to ask if he had a minute to talk to us about our struggles. We went to a private room, where we gave a brief overview of what we had been through the past few years in the infertility and adoption journey.

"What I don't understand," I explained, "is why we aren't blessed with a child when we continue to trust God? Why won't this desire for a baby go away if I'm not meant to have one? People keep telling me that I can handle all the things God has given me, but I see no reason to go on anymore. I can't handle one more miscarriage," I said, crying.

"What you're going through is lonely. A miscarriage is like a silent disease."

Pastor Tom got my undivided attention. What? Someone actually acknowledged how painful this journey was.

"No, I mean it. When people go through other health issues, they have all sorts of support groups and people praying for them. When you go through infertility and miscarriage or adoption loss, it's a silent disease. People don't know how to support you, say really stupid things, and as a result, you feel lonely."

I nodded, dumbfounded at his wisdom.

"When people tell you that you can handle all the things God has given you, they are wrong."

"What? Really? But everyone says that!"

"And everyone is wrong. The truth is that you can't handle all those things on your own, and instead, you must rely on God to get you through these trying times. You have two choices right now, and the consequences are huge. You can turn to God and trust him, or you can walk away. That's it. I hope and pray that you will lean on God as he will use all these heartaches for good someday. I know you can't see that now, but he will."

Crying, I muttered, "I just can't take much more. Why can't the desire go away, so I can just move on with my life?"

"Only God knows. You don't know the future but try to enjoy today. Instead of praying for a baby, pray for God's will and strength to accept whatever is meant to be. As hard as it is, try to find joy in your life."

I wanted peace and joy again. I wanted to accept the fact that God's will might not be for us to have kids any which way — a difficult fact to swallow without throwing up. I continued to ask God to take the desires of my heart away, a prayer I begged God to answer in the past. This time when I prayed, I truly meant it, and let go of the dream of being parents if that was indeed God's plan for our lives. Obviously, it wasn't my plan, and I needed help accepting this detour in my life if that's how it was going to be.

As we worked for acceptance of whatever God's will would be for us and as we went through the motions of trying to be happy again, Phil and I joined a new Bible study group through our church. When it was my turn to give a prayer request, I briefly shared our struggles with infertility as well as the pain of the adoption wait. I asked for prayers that God would be with us and clearly answer our prayers or show us His will and help us to accept it.

That night, a friendly blonde gal named Julie befriended me, telling me I reminded her of herself in her struggles for a second child. As a result, she ended up adopting a baby from foster care. Clearly, at a point in my life where I needed someone in town to talk to about this journey, God provided that person again. Julie reminded me of the importance of living in the moment — a lesson that would help me learn to find and experience joy again. I had to pay attention to the blessings I had in my life.

Days later, as I heard of another friend's pregnancy announcement, I felt desperately sad and betrayed by God yet again. Near my final breaking point, my husband came home from work that evening with an envelope that had my name on it. He said someone dropped it off at our hardware store. Slowly, I opened the envelope, a bit skeptical, yet read the following anyway:

One night I had a dream...
I dreamed I was walking along the beach with the Lord, and across the sky flashed scenes from my life.
For each scene, I noticed two sets of footprints in the sand; one belonged to me, and the other to the Lord.

When the last scene of my life flashed before us,
I looked back at the footprints in the sand.
I noticed that many times along the path of my life,
there was only one set of footprints.
I also noticed that it happened
at the very lowest and saddest times in my life
This really bothered me,
and I questioned the Lord about it.

"Lord, you said that once I decided to follow you,
You would walk with me all the way;
but I have noticed that during
the most troublesome times in my life,
there is only one set of footprints.
I don't understand why in times when I
needed you the most, you should leave me."

The Lord replied, "My precious, precious child.
I love you, and I would never,
never leave you during your times of trial and suffering.
When you saw only one set of footprints,
it was then that I carried you."

Tears welled up and quickly formed into a stream as I read the famous "Footprints" poem. So somehow, God put it in someone's heart to share this poem with me so I would know that God carried me when I felt all alone and abandoned again. I cried at the touching message, cried that I was still not pregnant, cried with a steady stream that God did not give me what I wanted, but deep down, felt at peace that God used someone else to let me know that He still cared and loved me. It wasn't until weeks later that we found out who sent us that note. A man whom we just met in the Bible study group said that God told him to write that note and drop it off — a miracle that I needed. God's timing was perfect, but because I was in the middle of the storm, I couldn't clearly see and comprehend that yet. I was depressed, stuck, and living in the past. To be at peace, I needed to live in that present moment of pain and trust that God walked in the storm alongside me, carrying and loving me all along.

PART V: God's Timing with Prayers Answered His Way

God never did answer my prayers for a biological child, but He surpassed my yearnings for a family in His own way, showing me that He had a plan all along. The author, Pablo Coelho, said it best in The Alchemist: "I love you because the universe conspired to help me find you." The journey proved to be one of faith, trust, and persistence in believing that God could bring us the children who were meant to be ours, as well as perform miracles that could not be medically explained in any way. And, perhaps it is through my children that I am reminded to have "faith like a child" as God talks through them too!

Chapter 18: Message Through a Bumper Sticker

Faith is the belief that your life will unfold as it was meant to even when it unfolds into something painful and difficult to navigate. Do I believe he has a plan? Yes. But that means I have to hold on to that belief even when the process is not easy or safe.
— *Rachel Hollis*

"This adoption wait is killing me. Do you realize that it's been over a year now since we have been officially waiting?" I said to Phil while driving.

"Really? I didn't realize it's been a year already."

"Didn't realize? Doesn't it feel like a lifetime of waiting? I'm so sick of this!"

"Hey, look in front of you," Phil said, intrigued by what he saw ahead of him.

"Where?"

"Right there. On that bumper sticker and license plate."

The pickup truck directly in front of us had a Texas license plate and a bumper sticker that read, "Someone in TEXAS Loves You." It just so happened that our adoption agency was in Texas, and I presumed that the person in Texas who loved me might be a birth mother and future child.

I laughed out loud. "What are the chances of that, especially when we live in Wisconsin! Oh my gosh. It's a sign for us — a sign to believe and not give up!"

This chance happening, which seemed purposeful, reassured me and gave me hope at another low point in our adoption journey. Phil, being the skeptic, said, "Please don't read into things, but I do think it's cool."

To me, the bumper sticker on a Texas license plate was a sign of hope from God just when I needed it. The very next day in March, my social worker, Rosa, emailed me, saying, "You need to pray continuously this morning as a birth parent is looking at your profile." I couldn't believe it. This MUST be the special match.

A few hours later, my cell phone rang with Rosa's number glaring. She never called, so I felt giddy and anxious, like a teenage girl who waited forever for Prince Charming to call.

"Hello," I said.

"Are you sitting down?" Rosa happily asked.

"Yes," I replied hesitantly.

"Guess what? Today is the day you've been waiting for! You have been picked by two very special birth parents who I'd call 'the all-American couple'. They are due in early October. Congratulations. Jo loved how active you both are and loved that special painting you made of the nursery which she saw in your scrapbook that you made. She loves music, art, and writing too."

"No way! No way! No way!" I screamed with disbelief. The call I waited so long for finally arrived. Now pregnant in a sense, I laughed to myself, thinking that the sign from God with the license plate and bumper sticker message was indeed true after all.

Even with our exciting news, we remained guarded. Being "pregnant" still meant we could "miscarry," or the birth parents could change their minds and decide to parent the child. Unfortunately, we had many red flags that the match could fall apart. As happy as I wanted to feel, the fear attacked us, making us concerned and cautious. The birth mother was young and had parents with professional jobs and a high economic status, which meant that they could afford to parent this child if they wanted to. In addition, she was only twelve weeks along — not far enough to be showing or feel a baby kick or even really bond with the little one yet. The social worker also shared with us that both of them did not tell their parents about the pregnancy. Once they found out, would the grandparents talk them out of adoption, wanting to help them raise the child? Besides those concerns, they chose to move into an apartment and use adoption to have their living expenses paid for the duration of the pregnancy. How were we to know if they were just pretending to be interested in adoption as a way to have many of their medical and living expenses paid for? If they changed their minds and decided to parent their child, which they had every right to do, they would not owe us one cent, and we'd be out at least $15,000-20,000.

With that price-tag, we hemmed and hawed over whether to accept this match. After waiting so long, though, how could we say no? Like inexperienced gamblers in Las Vegas, we did not know which hand to play, and every move proved to be risky. I wished I knew the answer to Kenny Roger's famous line, "You've got to know when to hold em, know when to walk away and know when to run."

I wondered if we should be running away.

On paper, all the signs pointed to not accepting the adoption match, but God kept giving us peace of mind every time we prayed, telling us to trust Him, to go ahead with this adoption. We felt connected to this couple, much like when I met Phil that first night at the zoo. When I looked at the pictures sent of the birth parents, I couldn't help but stare at the mother's eyes — I caught a privileged glimpse into her soul. I felt I knew her and loved her at first sight. She even sent pictures of her at different stages of her childhood. One particular picture looked just like me when I was four. In fact, my mom couldn't tell which was her and which was me. After seeing pictures of them, our decision became clear. Our baby would be here soon. Well, not soon enough. We still had a grueling six month wait, full of twists and turns.

The birth mother didn't want to talk on the phone, but she wanted to get to know us through email and texting. After accepting the match, our social worker gave each of us contact information. When I saw Jo's email in my inbox for the first time, my heart beat fast with excitement.

Hi!
I'm really happy that y'all decided to go with me. I was worried that the family I chose would for whatever reason decide to turn me down. I was wondering if you would like us to put a scrapbook together like the one y'all made for us? I loved seeing the colorful picture of animals you painted for this future baby's nursery. I'm sure he/she will love looking at it. The fact that you'd take the time to make that makes me feel like you'd be a really caring and loving mother.

We have lots of pictures that we can share with you as well, and Derek has his complete family tree with documents that date back hundreds of years that I thought maybe y'all would find interesting ... As for my family, my dad is a prosecutor and my mom a nurse. I have two older brothers, Jason, who is five years older than me, and Jimmy, who is eleven years older than me.

I've lived in the same house my entire life. My dad is from a small town in Indiana, and my mom is from Chicago. My dad went to Notre Dame and then transferred to Indiana University for graduate school, where he met my mom. I'm not sure why they chose to move to Texas, especially considering that all of their family lives in the Midwest. I spent a good portion of my childhood in Indiana. I love it there; it's pretty and the weather is amazing.

I love traveling. I love beaches, so Florida and California are top destinations. I would like to go backpacking in Europe one day. As you can obviously tell, I have a lot of things I want to accomplish with my life. I want to do a cross country road trip, go to college and get a degree in fine arts and, after college, I want to join the Peace Corps — why not? People these days live for 80 years or more. The Peace Corps is a two-year sacrifice. That is 1/40th of my life that I spend helping people in need). After that, I will backpack through Europe. I know that I will want to do even more as the years go on. So my raising a child at this point in my life would set me back. It's very difficult to travel with a child, and it's financially devastating to juggle a kid and school. So, that's why I decided to place my baby for adoption, and I can tell by y'all's scrapbook and the way you are so interested in Derek and me that you will give our baby a wonderful life, more than I could do myself.

Talk later,
Jo

We went back and forth with emails like this once or twice a week for most of the pregnancy. Everything seemed to be going well getting to know each other, and then out of nowhere, an email from her social worker surprised us when Jo was about seven months along.

Christine,
This is Colleen. Jo is overwhelmed and wants some space. Don't email her until she emails you, and when you write her, write her through me first, and I will give

her your messages when I see her for counseling. And one more thing you should know — Jo finally told her parents about the adoption, but the birthfather's parents still don't know. Take Care.

My mind spun in circles a mile a minute. So many questions bombarded my mind. I quickly called Colleen. "Hi, Colleen. This is Christine. Why is she overwhelmed? Is she changing her mind? Did I say something to set her off? If so, what did I do wrong? How did her parents react to finding out she is pregnant?"

"I don't know. For now, it's best to just give her some space. Hang in there. It's not uncommon for birth mothers to second guess themselves, especially when they are this far along."

Hanging up the phone, my body shook while my stomach rumbled. I wanted to throw up at the thought of losing a baby who felt destined to be ours. But reality slapped me in the face, reminding me that the little one developing in Jo's tummy was not ours and might never be. Again, nothing was in my control. For weeks, I went through the mixed motions of trying to prepare for the baby's arrival. I felt pure joy and excitement, but other times, I felt like a fraud. I wasn't a real mommy. I didn't have anything to show for it, and in a few months when the baby was due, he or she might not really be ours anyway.

Regardless of the mixed bag of emotions we dealt with, and because I've always been a planner, we needed to be ready, just in case this adoption did indeed happen. We did all we could to prepare — set up the nursery, had baby showers, read books on parenting, which only stressed me out more. I imagined most expectant moms felt excited when going through these preparatory steps, yet I felt cheated. I couldn't be happy because it didn't feel real, and I had to guard my heart in case the adoption failed. As most parents already know, so much of the learning happens on the job when the baby pees and poops on you, spits up on you, and screams at you. We wondered if we'd even get the chance to really learn those "fun" things.

During this time, I went back and forth on whether we

should get the nursery ready or not. Doing so felt emotionally painful. Not doing so made me feel unprepared and anxious. I couldn't win the tug of war inside my own mind. After discussing this with my best friend, Amy, she said, "Would you prepare the nursery and have a shower if you were pregnant?"

"Of course, why?"

"Then why wouldn't you do so for this child? Even when a person is pregnant, nothing is guaranteed. Things can still go wrong. Do your best to enjoy these special moments, and if the adoption falls through, deal with that then," Amy confidently said.

"I never thought of it that way. Okay, will you meet me at that baby store and tell me what stuff I have to register for?"

"I thought you'd never ask. Let's go tomorrow," Amy insisted.

Amy showed me the unfamiliar world of Babies R Us. I felt I needed a Cliff Notes version of which car seat, stroller, crib, highchair, baby bottle, etc. was best. And if the best meant four times the cost, did I really need that version? I didn't have time or energy to research all this like I normally would, and at that point, I just trusted my best friend's opinion having had three young children of her own. She could have written a book on the pros and cons of which items to buy, and I was grateful for her wisdom.

After registering, Amy and my new friend Jena from church insisted I have a baby shower and wouldn't take no for an answer. They ironically knew each other from college as Jena ended up marrying Amy's past boyfriend whom she dated for two years in high school. At first, that was strange for both of them, but they talked and ended up planning the shower together. Every time I told them no, Jena said, "You're paying enough for this adoption already and have spent so much money on your infertility journey. Please just let us shower you with baby presents. You deserve this. Your future baby deserves this."

"Okay, I guess," I said nervously.

"Don't guess. Trust that God will see this through," Jena said.

A few weeks later, my friends and family showered me with so much love. They had a cute jungle cake similar to the picture I painted for the nursery and one of those diaper and baby burp pad "cakes" with a stuffed monkey attached to it. Someone had carving talents and made a cute baby carriage out of a watermelon. At each place setting was a laminated bookmark with a Bible verse from Hebrews 10:23, saying, "Let us hold unswervingly to hope we profess, for he who promised is faithful." While I felt awkward celebrating without a belly full of baby, people surprised me and genuinely were happy for me. The Bible verse was true — I needed to have hope. All my family and friends may not have known the recent developments of how the birthmother became distant toward us. I didn't want to burst their bubble with Debbie Downer-type news and secretly hoped that none of that would come to fruition. The shower itself was surreal as I struggled to believe that an adoption placement would really happen. I learned through this journey over and over, though, to try and live in the present moment, so I kept telling myself to just enjoy the moment of hope and believe that this little baby would soon be ours, regardless of how difficult it was to do so. I tried my best to smile and put on a happy facade for everyone else. At times, when I opened a present and saw a cute little outfit that was so small it looked like it was for a baby doll, I forgot my facade and genuinely felt joy and hope.

After the shower, three weeks dragged on with no contact from Jo. I worried that Jo's parents would not support this adoption plan and instead, help her financially to parent this little one blossoming inside her. Sometimes the wait hurt more than the infertility dance that I did for years because this time, a live baby grew day by day, and I had no way of knowing if he was okay. I felt connected on a soulful level to this baby, yet at the same time, disconnected too because he wasn't growing inside of me. While I had everything ready to go, my heart still ached to know if I was really going to be this baby's mommy. I clung to my Bible verses on trust. In one dream, God reminded me, "Be still and know." As scared as I felt about losing this adoption match, I also had a sense of peace too when I listened to God. The mix of emotions reminded me of the highs and lows I endured with all my pregnancies and miscarriages.

During Jo's eighth month of pregnancy, a package arrived at my front door with her return address. I frantically opened up the box, wondering what she sent me, especially since she made no effort to talk to us in over three weeks. Inside, I saw an old faded white quilted baby blanket and with each square, a cute picture of a house or animal on it. Enclosed with the blanket was a letter:

Hi guys,

This was my baby blanket that my mom made for me. I always liked looking and playing on it when I was little. I'd pretend that the houses were a neighborhood, and my Barbies lived in them. I hope your baby will enjoy it as much as I did. I saw the pictures you posted from the baby shower. Your family seems nice, and I loved the watermelon carriage. All the baby clothes were cute too. I really liked the tiger outfit. It looks like I will be induced on September 29th. Let's plan to meet at my favorite barbecue restaurant the night before. See you then.

Love,
Jo

Overflowing with emotion, I called Phil at work. "Phil. Guess what? Jo sent us her baby blanket to give to the baby. She wouldn't do that if she were going to keep the baby, right? And she has a date set for being induced. We might just be parents after all," I quickly reported.

"Okay, that's great. Don't get too excited yet," Phil said matter-of-factly. While I wanted him to show more emotion like I did, I realized we are wired differently, and he had to guard his heart until he had solid reason to believe we would be parents for sure.

The last few weeks flew by, yet my world stopped to mourn when my beloved grandpa passed away from age-related issues at the age of 98 and a half years old. The last time I saw Grandpa, he told me, "Your son will be born in three weeks. I will be going to heaven and talking to God. I will tell him to watch over you, Phil, and your special baby boy. While I won't meet him on Earth, I hope I will see and meet him wherever he is." Grandpa dying reminded me of the circle of life. While he passed on, another baby was soon to be born. I felt comforted knowing that his love and wisdom would always be a part of me.

Meanwhile, Jo and I wrote a few more times back and forth discussing names. Having taught thousands of students for over two decades, I wanted a unique name, one to symbolize the special journey, and one that had no previous connotations. It had to be a two-syllable name as that would sound good with the two-syllable last name "Thoma". And finally, it had to feel right. I told her about how I wanted him to be named Noah. Jo replied, "I like the name Noah, but it's going to be really popular. I know so many already. This is going to be a special baby who needs a one-of-a-kind name. Any ideas?"

Surprisingly, I wasn't upset about trying out a different name. Noah teased me too many times coming and going whenever I thought I was pregnant with him. I needed a fresh start. As I scanned a baby book, the name Beckett just leaped off the page. That's it. That's his name I thought. I didn't even know much about the name, but it sounded perfect. I quickly wrote her back asking her opinion.

"Oh my. I love it. It's strong. And if people want to call him 'Beck' for short, it sounds tough sort of like the band, Beck. Have you heard of it?" Jo asked.

"I have. They were a good rock band! I think it sounds like a strong, unique name. Yay. He has a name!"

Three weeks later, the day to meet Jo and Derek at her favorite Texas barbecue restaurant finally arrived. Talk about nervous. What would we possibly talk about? What if they didn't like us? What if we came all this way from Wisconsin and spent a lot of time and money on this match for nothing? What if they changed their minds? I reminded myself that she needed loving parents to adopt her baby as much as we needed her baby to become parents. We wanted to please each other, yet Jo maintained all the power in this decision, which made me feel insecure and anxious for our meeting.

Right before the most important meeting of our lives, we had a little time to spare, so we checked out a nearby gift shop. As I browsed through all the souvenirs, postcards, and signs of which many said, "Don't Mess with Texas," I stopped dead in my tracks and started crying when I saw a familiar bumper sticker. It read, "Someone in TEXAS loves you." Unbelievable timing! I quickly bought two of these bumper stickers — one for the birth mother and one for the baby's special scrapbook that I planned to make.

While some might say seeing that bumper sticker was merely a coincidence, it was confirmation for me that someone in Texas did love me — our birth mother, our future baby, and in return, we loved the birth parents with a bond that only those who have gone through an adoption could understand. We created a special triangle of love. With this sign from above, my nerves eased, and we confidently walked into our first meeting. It felt like the ultimate interview, and we were ready to give them a special bumper sticker and a heartfelt story of love and gratitude.

Seeing Jo and Derek walk through the door of the restaurant made our hearts flutter. She glowed, looking both peaceful and happy. I couldn't get over how much Jo and Derek shared similarities to how Phil and I looked in terms of height, build, complexion, hair and eye color. I started to daydream about what the baby might look like and imagined how it might even look a lot like us. And it was surreal to think that the baby inside her belly would be outside the next day and that we'd be hopefully holding a newborn. Like old friends meeting for the thousandth time, we ate and talked openly about everything from favorite foods, music, travel, school, work, and dreams of the future. By 8 p.m., Jo needed to leave to check into the hospital for her scheduled induction. As we hugged, she said she'd see us tomorrow at the hospital.

The next morning, we met Jo's parents in the elevator. "You must be Christine and Phil," Jo's mom Sara said.

"Yes, how did you know?"

"We were at the restaurant last night. We were around the corner, spying on you. Sorry about that, but we just wanted to make sure you two were okay for this baby," Sara explained.

"Oh. I hope we passed the test," I said jokingly, but also somewhat serious.

"Just promise me one thing."

"What's that?" Phil asked.

"Promise me that you will always love this baby and that you will give him a good education and raise him as a Christian?" Sara expressed.

"That's no problem. We already love him and belong to a strong Christian church. We both value education. Christine's a high school English teacher," Phil said.

"That's right. Jo told me that. Well, you guys will make great parents. Congrats, and please stay in touch."

A few hours later, I saw them again with both Jo and Derek in Jo's hospital room. Jo had on a Harry Potter movie while her dad, an attorney, read the newspaper. Jo's mom shared more family history with me, letting me know that they were of Irish and German descent. I took lots of notes as they told us stories of their family — that Jo's brothers enjoyed playing baseball, that all did well in school, that they had one relative die of cancer and another a heart attack. I wanted to know everything I could from them, so that I'd have it all to share someday in case we'd ever lose touch.

God must have hand-picked the hospital staff on call that late September night when Beckett was born. They put Jo in one room with the door open and had us next door. We were able to watch the contractions on a monitor above us and heard Beckett's first cry as he entered the world. Overjoyed, we laughed and cried at Beckett's first tears, knowing there would be many more to come. The doctor who delivered him had a husband who was adopted, and two of the delivery nurses had siblings who were adopted as well. Knowing the importance of bonding, they broke their hospital's rules by allowing us to hold and care for Beckett five minutes after he was born. They even set us up with our own hospital room, which we stayed in for three nights for free.

The moment the nurse brought Beckett for me to meet him is one that will be etched in my memory forever. The minute I held Beckett for the first time and looked into his alert ocean blue eyes, I remembered the night I met Phil because that meeting always felt meant to be as well. Beckett and I had an immediate soul connection; I knew him, so much that I wondered if he could be the same soul who came and went all those times I was pregnant. At that moment, I realized God intended us to be parents to this special soul all along. A biological connection did not matter; we were all in love, and we were meant to be a family. I couldn't believe that I ever questioned our going down the adoption path to become parents.

Knowing in my heart that God brought us the soul of who we were meant to parent, immediately healed and wiped out any longing for a biological child. I never thought that day would come, but God was faithful. For years, I prayed for God to take the desire for a child away, so I could feel joy again. I could not understand why that desire remained until I held Beckett for the first time. Beyond grateful for this automatic love connection, I couldn't stop smiling as I held Beckett and stared into his pretty blue-green eyes. I knew we were meant to find one another. It seemed to be destiny.

As much love and joy that we immediately felt in the birth of Beckett, the next day, the hands of reality grabbed us, causing us extreme sadness and guilt. As I thought about Jo and Derek in the room next door, I realized that our gain was their loss. With this jolting realization, I cried. Tears of happiness quickly morphed into tears of guilt, shame, and resentment for this unfair situation that most people never have to experience. It was like wishing an organ donor would die, so that your loved one could have their organ to live. I didn't want anyone to feel such a heart wrenching loss. The whole situation was bittersweet and unfair. As I kept crying and my heart throbbed, Jo and Derek knocked on the door.

"Why are you crying?" Jo asked, confused.

"I was just thinking about how I'm so grateful for you guys, but how guilty I feel adopting your baby," I sobbed.

"You all will be excellent parents. When I chose you guys to adopt Beckett, I knew that it meant I can't keep him, even though I love him too and wish I could. Don't be sad," Jo selflessly said.

Derek added, "I went home to get this for Beckett. It was my teddy bear when I was little. I want him to have it to remember us by."

I tried to hold back my tears, but as I started to hyperventilate and shake, Jo hugged me for just a few seconds. "I love you, and thank you," I said.

"We love you too. We will be signing the termination of parental rights tomorrow and going home after that. Congrats on your new son."

"Beckett will always know about you and how much you love him. Please stay in touch. I hope we can see you when we come back to Texas to finalize his adoption in court in six months," I pleaded.

"Of course. We will miss y'all so much. Please send lots of pictures."

"We will," Phil said with tears in his eyes too. If anyone came into hospital room 132 that evening, they might have thought someone died, but all those tears were the result of lots of love. When they left that night, I wondered if we'd ever see them again, and that thought felt like a hole in my heart. It was a complex connection, but one that would be with us forever.

The next morning, our social worker, Colleen came to the hospital. "Awwww. Beckett is so cute! Congrats, guys. I'm so happy for you. Jo and Derek signed the termination of parental rights papers. Beckett is yours. You are free to go anywhere you want as long as you stay in Texas for the next two weeks until we get the interstate paperwork done for you to go back to Wisconsin. We will be in touch. Take care." A minute later, the nurse came in, gave us the discharge papers and made sure we knew how to work the car seat before we left.

After the nurse left, Phil and I looked at each other with confusion.

"What do we do now?" Phil asked.

After a slight pause, I joked, "I guess we drive away and live happily ever after."

"This is so weird. After all we've been through, here he is. This is real."

"I know. It's so hard to believe. I don't even know how to feel. Driving twenty-two hours down here, meeting the birthparents and Jo's parents, waiting for Beckett to be born, then holding him for the first time, and then the emotional goodbye. I'm so exhausted, yet ecstatic and excited too," I said.

"I know, but he's finally here. Enjoy this moment. Let's get going. This will be Beckett's first car ride," Phil said as he smiled.

As we walked out of the hospital, I sort of felt as though I was stealing a baby because it felt too good to be true. I kept reminding myself that we were real parents. Finally.

From Austin, TX, we drove to San Antonio to stay with some family and friends while we waited for Wisconsin and Texas social workers to approve the interstate compact. As we drove, I kept turning back to stare in awe at Beckett. He looked like a little angel as he slept so peacefully, and his face glowed from the light within. He truly was a gift from God.

Our first stop included a visit to the Alamo. Why not give Beckett a little history lesson right away? At a gift shop nearby to get some souvenir postcards, a store clerk said, "What a cute baby. How old is he? He's so small."

"He's three days old today," I responded proudly.

"Oh wow. You look fabulous for just having a baby, and he looks just like you," the clerk said.

Phil nudged me and mumbled, "Tell her."

"Thank you so much," I said happily.

Walking out, Phil said, "Why didn't you tell her that we adopted him?"

"Because we don't have to. After all we've been through, I'm just going to let myself have that compliment," I chuckled.

When we were matched for this adoption, we rowed along in a deep fog and could not see the outcome, but somehow, we believed things would work out. Believing in God's goodness and power when we couldn't see through the fog in the storm taught us what faith really meant.

A few years before Beckett's birth, while waiting almost a year for an adoption match, I made some pottery as an outlet for my frustration. For some reason, I felt compelled to write the word "believe" on the vase I made and told myself that I would try to trust that this adoption would eventually happen.

Around that same time, my friend, Jena, gave me a special red stone for Christmas, and low and behold, it had the word "believe" written on it. She explained how she often held this stone during her painful wait for child number two, whom she also adopted. That simple gift was one of my favorites as it reinforced the lesson that God wanted me to learn. I needed to believe and trust in Him and His timing. She also gave me this special verse to ponder from Hebrews 12:1-3: "And let us run with perseverance the race marked out for us, fixing our eyes on Jesus." Stuck on mile twenty-three in the greatest marathon of my life, I tried to believe that Jesus would either bless us with a child or help me accept that it was not God's will for us to be parents.

So, you're probably wondering, what is the point of this tangent and how does it relate to the name Beckett? Hold on, dear friends … I come full circle. After naming our sweet boy, Beckett, another friend wrote me after having done some name research and said, "Oh, I see why you named him Beckett because one of the meanings of his name is "to believe".

Unbelievable coincidence — but on second thought, it was just another confirmation of how God had His hand in helping us name him. We did not know what his name meant when we named him, but I was given signs all along to believe, and then come to find out that one meaning of his name means to believe. It all made perfect sense.

Chapter 19: Adjustment to Parenthood

There is no such thing as a perfect parent, so just be a real one.
— *Sue Atkins*

Two weeks after Beckett's birth on a pretty autumn day while we waited in Texas, the Wisconsin office finally gave us the approval to go back to our home state. Woohoo! Willie Nelson's song, "On the Road Again" could not have been truer as we "just couldn't wait." We were on the road again, headed to home sweet home with our precious baby riding with us — so surreal. The normal nineteen-hour drive took us much longer as we had to stop every three hours to feed and change Beckett. It amazed me how quickly those hours flew by, and little did I know that Beckett's routine of eating, pooping, and sleeping every three hours around the clock would become mine too.

You'd think that after waiting almost a decade for our baby, driving home would be easy, but I wished we were instantly transported home. I could hardly wait for my family and friends to finally meet our special angel. As Beckett slept peacefully in the backseat, I kept turning around to look at him to remind myself that being a mother was real. And then he reassured me by opening his light blue eyes. He gazed into mine with a smile that seemed meant just for me, reminding me that he was real, that I'm his mommy, and that our finding each other was meant to be all along.

After the long drive home and ready to start our lives as a family of three, our kind neighbors welcomed us with a large congratulations sign hung on our garage door as well as balloons and special cute outfits from many families and friends. Like a celebrity, everyone wanted to meet Beckett. We beamed with genuine happiness and felt proud to show him off. But first, we insisted that everyone wash and sanitize their hands. Of course, we read up on all the horrible things that could happen if Beckett became ill with a fever those first eight weeks. No way were we going to let him get sick on our watch. Some people laughed and thought we were kidding until Phil asked them to put their hands out while he meticulously sanitized their hands.

After a month of a steady flow of visitors, life became routine, and I enjoyed a four-month maternity leave from work. Here's where I'd like to tell you we lived happily ever after, and that being a new mother was a dream come true. And it was. And it wasn't. I felt a tug of war between wanting and needing space and freedom and between wanting to be with and care for Beckett every second. I tried my best to adjust to this alien world of motherhood, but truth be told, I had no idea what I was doing and falsely believed that everyone else did. That lack of experience, especially as a perfectionist coupled with a new routine of little sleep and new anxieties obsessing over if Beckett ate and slept enough, met milestones, rolled over correctly, had enough tummy time just about drove me crazy. I'd wake up in the middle of the night to check if he slept okay. With his reflux, I constantly worried if he'd choke and die. When he came down with his first cold and ear infection, I panicked, wondering if he'd make it through. With piles of laundry and no time to shower or maintain the house as well as I did before Beckett was born, I wondered who I was. What happened to me? Was I good enough to be a mom?

To connect with other moms, I joined a MOPS (Mothers of Preschoolers) group at church. It didn't help. As they talked about their difficulties in recovering from childbirth, I couldn't relate. As much as I wanted to leave the scars of infertility behind me, and as happy as I felt being a mother, the wounds of infertility reopened. Even when some of the ladies complained about their child's piercing cries, lack of sleep, and not having time to themselves, I secretly related, but an overwhelming sense of guilt stopped me from connecting and sharing the fact that I felt the exact same way. How could I complain after all I did to become a mother? For so many years, I prayed and pleaded with God for a child. Having that prayer answered, I felt I didn't have the right to complain at all about anything. In an identity crisis, I tried to focus on how grateful I felt for having the opportunity to put on the mommy hat for once. Being a new mother was the most exhausting time of my life, but also the most rewarding — such a paradox of two polar opposite feelings. But that's what it was, and nothing could have prepared me for that.

It took time for me to believe in my heart that I was a real parent, and just like everyone else, I had a right to complain. As I encountered ignorant people who'd ask intrusive questions about

Beckett's adoption, it didn't take long for my protective mother bear side to shine through. So often I heard people say, "How wonderful that you saved a child. Beckett is truly blessed." I never thought that way. We weren't saviors rescuing some poor, needy child. We wanted a child to parent. Adoption was one wonderful opportunity to achieve our dream of parenthood. While Beckett may be blessed too, we were the ones truly blessed.

Another time, a well-intentioned friend asked, "What happened to the real mother? How could she give up her baby?"

I replied, "I am the real mother. You must mean his birthparents. And the birthmother loves Beckett too. Her placing him for adoption shows how much she loves him." Unfortunately, comments and negative stereotypes of the birthparents were made a lot, and they subconsciously poked at my heart, making me doubt my worth as a mother. People didn't seem to view me as the "real" mother. When I went back to work, the work/life balance with my endless strive for perfection created months of sleepless nights as my mind ran overtime with to do lists. I thought I could no longer do anything well as the demands of parenting, teaching, and being a wife pulled me in every direction. I needed a compass home to find myself again.

To add to my guilt, I received a letter from Jo which read:

Hi guys:

I received the pictures of Beckett and coincidentally on the same day that he turned one month old. I can barely take in the reality that just over a month ago, I gave birth to a little boy, and for nine months before that, I held him inside me. So when I received those pictures, I just felt really sad and cried for a while. Derek was upset too, but he mostly tried to hold and comfort me. I miss Beckett so much. I think about him every day, and sometimes I swear I still feel him kicking inside my belly. I feel like a part of me is missing and even though I know how happy he is with you, and how happy you are with him, I still think

*about being a mom and having someone else to take care
of beside myself. Derek told me that I bottle up my feelings
too much, but I feel better typing this up for you, and I
hope you understand, and that I didn't upset you or
anything. I'm also going to send you the sonograms for
you to have. It's funny what you said about playing the
Doors and how Beckett started dancing. I put headphones
on my belly for him to listen to them several times. I also
did with the Mars Volta and the Beatles too. Talk soon.*

Love,
Jo

    Hearing Jo say all that made my head and heart throb, but at
the same time, I felt grateful that she was comfortable sharing her
feelings with me. I just didn't know how to feel. Did she regret her
decision to place her baby with us? Would she come up to
Wisconsin and try to get Beckett back? I didn't really think so, but
for a minute, that nightmare scenario entered my mind. A few days
later, I hesitantly attended another MOPS meeting. A speaker there
described her lack of work and life balance, saying, "You have to
take care of yourself first. If mama isn't well, no one is." An ideal
thought for sure. I kept thinking that I didn't have the time to put me
first, and if I did so, everything else would fall apart.

    That night after many months of silence, God talked to me in
my dreams, saying, "You are enough, and remember, you are and
were meant to be Beckett's mother." As tears rolled down my cheek,
I remembered how God orchestrated the whole adoption, and how I
knew God used Jo's body to bring me Beckett whose soul I always
knew before as Noah. In a book I read at the time, sociologist and
author Brene Brown stated, "Shame is the most powerful master
emotion. It is the fear that we are not good enough." I smiled full-
heartedly knowing I was Beckett's mother and always would be. I
vowed to never doubt again. From that point on, I didn't care what
others thought. It didn't matter. What mattered was that I needed to
lower my expectations and no longer feel guilt or shame that I wasn't
good enough as a mom. I was, indeed, enough! A great day meant
that Beckett was fed, bathed, and safe. In order to rejuvenate my
soul, I started to practice self-care by taking time to exercise, write,
talk to friends, and spend time in nature. If I needed to complain

about the demands of motherhood and life, I did. No more guilt. With my cup full, I had more to give to everyone else, especially Phil and Beckett. With the whirlwind adjustment those first five months, I found myself again. If I wasn't already, I was determined to be a badass mom. By living in the present moment again, I enabled myself to enjoy all the mundane routines of life.

When Beckett was six months old, we went back to Texas to finalize his adoption. Jo and Derek invited us to eat dinner at her parents' house, which was much bigger than ours back home. I'm not sure why that surprised me, but maybe because it made me think again that her family appeared to have the means to care for Beckett. This was the first time we saw them since our blubbering, sad goodbyes to each other in the hospital when Beckett was just two days old. Knowing lots of pictures would be taken, I dressed Beckett in the cutest outfit I could find. He sported colorful overalls with a royal blue shirt, and a matching plaid hat that had a cute little monkey on it. Jo's mom, excited to play the grandma role, showered us with bags of gifts including Texas cowboy boots, Ralph Lauren shirts, lots of matching outfits, tons of board books, and bath toys. I worried we wouldn't have room for it all in our suitcase, but somehow, we made it work. And oh, my goodness — the ribs! Jo's dad, Beckett's biological grandpa, made the best smoked dry ribs we've ever had. One of my favorite memories of the night was when Beckett sat next to Derek while he lovingly played both the guitar and harmonica for him. As we sadly said our goodbyes, we wondered if we'd see them again, but Jo and her dad said they'd be in Chicago in three months to visit relatives. They promised they'd call us to meet them.

They were true to their word. When Beckett was nine months old, we drove two hours to Chicago to meet them, take in the sights around Navy Pier, and enjoy some seafood at Bubba Gump's Shrimp Factory. Jo took a ton of pictures and seemed genuinely happy, holding and playing with Beckett. Since they come to the Midwest yearly to visit relatives, I didn't think that hug in Chicago would be our last. We didn't hear from Jo or her family until Beckett turned five. Out of the blue, Jo private messaged me on Facebook, saying,

"I know I have been missing in action, but please know I love Beckett, and because I miss and love him so much, I needed to distance myself. It's hard to believe that Beckett is turning five. Can I please send him a gift?" My heart ached those years she did not stay in touch. Of course, she could contact Beckett. My heart smiled that she wanted to. A few days later, a box arrived with a t-shirt of the Austin Film Society, where she worked and a special card that read:

To my little Beckett,

Wishing you oceans of fun on your Birthday! Five years is huge! Not a day goes by where I don't think of you and how I held you on your first day of life. Happy Birthday, Beckett. I know I'll see you soon.

Love,
Jo

While we haven't seen or heard from Jo or her family since then, we hold hope that she will contact us again one day when she is ready. We know she loves Beckett, and that her distance is a needed boundary for her at this point. The door is always open for her.

Surprisingly, after Beckett turned one, I received a phone call from a lady named Missy, Derek's mom and Beckett's biological grandmother, who also lives in Texas. Supposedly, she found pictures of Beckett that I sent to Derek and went ballistic when she found out she had a grandson that she did not know about.

"I'm just in shock that Beckett exists and that Derek did not tell me. He's very cute and looks so happy with you guys. Please, can we be part of your lives? Honestly, had I known about him before the adoption happened, we would have tried to talk him out of it. I would have raised him if Derek couldn't," Missy pleaded.

I almost dropped the phone and didn't know what to say. After a dramatic pause, I said, "Well, I'm really glad that you didn't know about it then!"

"I'm sorry. I shouldn't scare you. I'm just so in shock. I just have to meet him! Can Ashley, Derek's sister, and I drive up and see him? Would that be okay?"

"Um, sure. Let me figure out some dates and get back to you."

A month later, Missy came to our home where we sat outside and had a delicious barbecue. They checked us out, looked at our house, and asked us lots of questions about our dreams, hobbies and future goals. It felt a little like an interview, and I wanted to point out that we already had the job, but I went along with entertaining them as they were Beckett's relatives. They played with Beckett in his sandbox and swung him in his favorite swing. Missy gave him a special teddy bear and a note saying she loved him, a gift he still cherishes to this day. Some of my friends couldn't believe I even let her in our house since she said that she would have adopted Beckett and seemed irked that he existed without her knowledge. For some reason, God told me that it would be okay and that she needed to see him to understand how our family was meant to be. A few weeks after her visit, I received a thank you note in the mail from Missy, saying:

Dear Thoma family,

Thank you so much for letting us meet your family and especially sweet little Beckett. As we drove away, I told Ashley that I was not sad because I know that Beckett is a gift from God and meant to be yours, and you guys are excellent parents. Beckett will have a great life with you all.

I'm so proud of Derek for doing an adoption placement, and maybe he understood something I didn't. If I knew about their pregnancy and adoption plan, I may have ruined what God intended all along. Anyway, I feel some closure now but would still like to be part of Beckett's life through Facebook and whatever you are comfortable allowing. Thank you and please stay in touch!

Love,
Missy

As I read that heart-felt note, I smiled and said to myself, "Thank you, God. Thank you for Beckett." We sure dodged a bullet having this adoption go as planned.

Chapter 20: Waiting on God Again with Adoption #2

Nothing is wasted. Every single moment is preparing you for the next...all of it is growing you for the person you are becoming, for a future you can't even imagine.
— *Rachel Hollis*

The journey to our first son, Beckett, taught me great lessons on how to trust God and have persistence like nothing else in my life could have taught me. Feeling I mastered those lessons, we thought adoption number two would be a much easier journey, which we decided to start immediately after Beckett's adoption was finalized six months after his birth. Again, we needed to go through the exhausting and tedious process of making a scrapbook, from which the birthparents would choose us, and fill out loads of paperwork and interview questions from social workers in addition to having our home inspected and our backgrounds checked. I'm not sure why I thought this process would be any easier. What were we thinking? As months and years went by, I started to wonder if Beckett would ever have a sibling. When we hit the second year of waiting to get picked, which meant Beckett was two and a half years old, many of my friends announced how they were pregnant with their second or third baby. Was I reliving the same nightmare all over again? Deep inside, my soul grew weary, and I found myself again questioning God. Why did wanting another child need to be so trying? Why couldn't we just be blessed already with a second child? And why did I need to be tested again on the lessons of trust and persistence? I thought I mastered them, but I soon realized that lessons sort of recycle themselves like playing a higher level in a video game. You master one level but get tested on the next. Adoption number two proved to be another challenging test through a category five storm.

After two years of waiting for our second adoption, my husband and I decided to metaphorically give up. We were still in the adoption pool, waiting, but resolved to be happy with what we had. If Beckett didn't have a sibling, then that was what was meant to be. We had each other, our little Beckett, good jobs, our health, and our family and friends. We were blessed beyond measure. In many ways, I felt guilty being angry with God that I wanted another child. And I'm not saying that giving up this dream for child number two was easy. It wasn't. We had to grieve the loss of the baby we planned on. Since the adoption match wasn't moving at all, and rather than dwelling on what we didn't have, we tried to appreciate and find joy in what we did have, which meant to start living in the present moment and allow ourselves to feel joy again. It wasn't fair to Beckett or to us to be living a life void of joy, a lesson we learned before in our journey to adopt Beckett. We applied this lesson more quickly this time around. Beckett allowed us both to find our inner child again and enjoy life. I'm not sure who had more fun when he was two years old and we drove out to Pennsylvania to take Beckett to Sesame Place, a magical amusement and water park with all the Sesame Street characters, including my favorite — Cookie Monster. Seeing the joy and excitement on Beckett's face as he had fun experiencing his first vacation as well as other simple family outings to museums, zoos, and parks slowly made any pain related to infertility and adoption fade away. We had dreams and a whole life ahead of us. The time had come to make our dreams a reality.

Shortly after Beckett was born, we bought a little plot of land on a very small lake with hopes to build our dream home. For years, we drove by this pristine and tranquil spot, wishing we could buy it someday, but for at least six years, it was way out of our price range even as we watched the price come down year after year. One day, I had a gut feeling that we should check this land out again. As we arrived at the lot, we noticed there were only two lots left out of the original ten to purchase. We made a few phone calls and found that the price was finally at the lowest point it would ever be, which luckily for us, now happened to be affordable and a good deal, considering other lots throughout the city. Within a few days, we put in an offer and couldn't believe that our dream home would soon be a reality. Ideally, we wanted to wait to build after adoption number two came. But since time continued to pass us by, we seized the opportunity to build before the interest rates climbed even higher.

In April of 2013, we met with a builder that we researched and talked with for the past year and signed a contract to build. The very next day, I received a call from Carrie, our social worker. Can you guess what happened next? Yep, after giving up and moving on, we were picked to adopt a baby boy who was due in four weeks.

Four weeks! Can you believe it? God certainly had a sense of humor. We just moved forward, thinking the adoption would never happen, and as a result, we put our house on the market and started to build a new one. We had to laugh at how God's timing was not always ours, but how could we complain? A baby was on the way!

Ecstatic that we'd have another son to love, we happily welcomed the surprising and awesome news. That week, we met the birth parents and birth-grandparents for the first time at a local pizza place only thirty minutes from our home. Much like meeting Beckett's birth family, our stomachs rumbled, and nausea overcame us out of pure nervousness, but as we walked in to meet them, God whispered to me, "Just be yourself, and don't forget that I'm in charge here." I smiled inside and figured that if they didn't like us, then their baby boy was not meant to be our son.

Because this adoption match happened so quickly toward the end of Amanda's pregnancy, we didn't have any pictures of the birthparents or letters from them beforehand, so meeting Amanda and Danny for the first time was like going on a blind date. Spotting them in the restaurant, I quickly noticed both their thin frames and how young, athletic and attractive they were. Amanda had long thin brown hair with cute freckles and an adorable dimple. Danny had a tan complexion, was rather tall, around 6 foot one, with dark wavy hair and brown eyes that invited you in and made you feel like you knew him before. Talking to them and their parents was comfortable, like we had been friends and known them all for years. We wanted to know everything about them. What were their favorite subjects in school? What sports and hobbies did they enjoy? What were their dreams for their futures? As we looked at the cute couple and learned about how much we all had in common, we imagined what the little boy inside of Amanda's belly might look like. We knew he'd be special and loved.

The interview was in no way one way, however. They asked several questions too. Patty, Danny's mom who was maybe only five or six years older than me and who could have been a model with her perfect complexion and wavy shoulder length blonde hair, looked us straight in the eyes, asking in a confident and no-nonsense tone, "Will you allow us to have an open adoption? It's really important that this little boy stay in all of our lives. We understand you have family too and don't want to be intrusive, but we want to have a relationship with him as he grows up."

Trying not to feel intimidated, I responded, "Yes. That's actually what we want. It's what's best for him. We wanted an open adoption with Beckett and stayed in touch with his birthmother for almost the whole first year, but then it became too hard for her. We are sad that we don't hear from her more."

"Okay, great. That means a lot," Patty said, smiling.

Danny chimed in, "Have you thought about any names?"

"I was going to ask you about that. I'm pretty picky since I'm a teacher and don't want any name of a student whom I've taught before. I was thinking of Gavin Daniel. Gavin because it sounds like a strong name. I picture someone athletic with it. Daniel because my best friend's name was Dan (he died unfortunately), my brother's name is Dan, and your name is Dan," I said.

"Oh, I love that name!" Danny said.

"Me too," Amanda added with a smile.

"That's great," Patty said. "My fiance's name is Dan too. Great name!"

I was touched that the name we were considering meant something for them too. The meeting felt comfortable and unforgettable. They asked more questions about our jobs, how we met, what religion we practiced. They were happy to hear that raising Gavin to be a strong Christian was important to us. Overall, we had a memorable first meeting and a special bond formed that is still present to this day in our open adoption. As we left the parking lot, Phil saw Danny's mom give a thumbs up to the expecting couple. We won the grandparents' approval, and our hearts beamed with joy and excitement that things looked positive for this adoption match.

Approximately four weeks later, while shopping at an outlet mall, my phone rang. It was Gavin's birth mom, Amanda. "Christine, I'm in labor," she said calmly. I wondered how she could sound so calm at a time like this.

"Um, really? Oh my God. What's that mean? Do you want us to come?" What a stupid question. How could I have even asked that? I didn't have a manual on how to respond when my soon- to-be adopted baby was about to be born.

"Yes! Baby should be here any time. Come when you can, and see you soon."

"Okay. Um, good luck, and we'll get there as fast as possible."

Thoughts invaded my mind quicker than I could process them. We were an hour and a half away from the hospital, and we had to find someone to take care of Beckett. We needed to pack our things yet too. At that exact moment, I needed to check out and get out of the long line at the Gap. Excited, I shouted out loud, "I'm having a baby!" People looked at me a bit strangely as I wasn't large in the belly, but then I added, "Oh, it's through adoption. My baby is going to be born soon. I need to go." As they all yelled, hugged and cheered for me, they motioned me to cut to the front as the line of twelve people clapped and high-fived me. It was like a scene out of a movie.

Fast forward a few hours — Gavin was born as planned, healthy, and cute as could be with his dark brown eyes, and two adorable little dimples. Unlike Beckett's birth parents who wanted us to oversee him from the start, Gavin's wanted to have him in their room most of the time. In addition, they had many of their relatives and close friends come to meet him. In the crazy world of adoption, that's a big red flag — any time birth parents have family and friends come to meet their baby, it can be a warning sign that they bonded and may want to parent the child. With our protective armor on, we couldn't let ourselves get too emotionally close to Gavin for our own psychological safety. In hindsight, I felt a deep sadness and guilt that the circumstances did not allow for us to bond right away.

The next day, the neonatologist came to talk to us about Gavin's droopy lower right lip. We noticed it too, but assumed it from his natural birth, which had to be a lot of work. Of course, things could get smushed along the way. Little did we know. When Gavin cried, his lower right lip sagged. Later, the doctors referred to it as "asymmetrical crying face syndrome." A syndrome? That couldn't be good. That sounded serious. "Sorry, but we are going to have to run a series of tests to see if there are other things wrong with him," the neonatologist stated matter-of-factly.

Tests? Other things wrong? What? My mind raced as my anxiety shook me up and creeped through every vein in my body. "Christine, don't worry about anything until we have something to worry about," Phil assured me. I prayed to God about it but didn't hear anything back. Feeling out of control and scared, all we could do was pray that all would be okay and if not, to help give us the strength to get through it. We had no control over any of this. I wished I were wired like Phil who remained calm in the middle of the storm again.

The next day, the neonatologist came with some results. "Well, I'm glad that he has no trouble swallowing his food or taking a bottle. Babies with this syndrome often have that issue. He did fail his hearing test in his left ear, and he has a small hole in his heart that needs to be checked out. I want you to follow up with a pediatric cardiologist as well as with a pediatric geneticist."

"Why? What does that mean? What else could be wrong?"

"Please don't worry until there is a reason. We just need to check everything and make sure we didn't miss something."

"Um, you need to tell me what other things you may have missed; if you don't tell me, I'll Google it and get scared, so you might as well tell me the truth of what you are looking for now." Gosh, it sounded like I held this doctor hostage with my demands for information. What could I say? I felt desperate, and knowledge was power.

With a sigh and a look like he had dealt with type A parents before, the neonatologist reported, "Sometimes when babies have this syndrome, it's a sign that other things are wrong too. Sometimes there are learning delays or physical malformations of the lungs, kidneys, and heart. We just want everything checked out to be sure he doesn't have any of those issues."

As the neonatologist said these words, I felt locked inside some strange, foggy dream. My body froze as anger and bitterness overcame me at the unfairness of the situation. We had already suffered so much in our journey to become parents. Couldn't God just bless us with a healthy child? Was that too much to ask at this point? It hadn't even crossed my mind that our baby, who wasn't even legally ours yet, could have serious and lifelong health issues. I didn't sign up for this. I needed a reset button. Dealing with a newborn who needed so much care did not match my vision for a happy family life. In a haze of fog over lack of sleep, anxiety, and fear, I couldn't believe the cards we were dealt.

A day later, the doctor gave us the okay to take Gavin home

and start our new life as a family of four. Seeing Beckett meet his little brother for the first time was perhaps one of the most heart-warming experiences I've ever witnessed. As Gavin sat all snug in his car seat upon arrival, Beckett darted out to see him in the foyer with his little Elmo doll in hand. "Here, Gavin. This is my favorite stuffed animal. You can use him to help you sleep." At first, Beckett treated Gavin as a precious new toy. He wanted to play ball with him and hold and feed him. He insisted on wearing the same outfits as him and put his arm around Gavin asking for their picture to be taken. A proud big brother, Beckett bonded quickly with him, laughing at his every move even when Gavin pooped and made the entire room need to clear out. "Gavin went poopy," Beckett laughed. That was just the start of future boy talk.

Overjoyed that Beckett appeared to have some type of soul connection with Gavin, we didn't have time to worry about all the what ifs with Gavin's unique diagnosis or bond how I wanted to. We had a new home being built, which needed to be babysat daily, checking on contractors and making sure every detail was done to perfection. Our current home was up for sale and had showings all the time. I had to constantly clean in a matter of minutes to make our house look like a two-year old and newborn did not live there with toys scattered all around. We both worked full time. This nonstop busy routine was a recipe for tears, sleepless nights, and pure craziness.

Meanwhile, even though bonding still proved challenging, a motherly instinct overpowered me with baby Gavin, and I wanted to get as many answers as I could to help him, as well as cross each worry off my list as quickly as I could for my own sanity. First stop, the ENT to have his hearing retested. Left ear: failed. Needed to retest three weeks later. Next stop, the pediatric cardiologist. Results — Gavin still had a hole in his heart that needed to be rechecked in a few weeks. If it didn't heal on its own, he'd need surgery to repair. Final stop: the pediatric geneticist. Results —a malformed kidney showed on the ultrasound. Again, we had an appointment to come back in four weeks to see if he could outgrow that on his own. In addition, they ran many genetic tests, which would take six weeks for results letting us know if Gavin was a carrier for any major chromosomal abnormalities. So far, the results were not in our favor. The geneticist said that "over ninety percent of babies with asymmetrical crying face syndrome usually have other markers for things wrong, but the severity of what's wrong varies greatly."

Heartbroken and lost, I cried, "Why, God? Please perform a miracle and heal Gavin. Please." Exhausted, I turned to my journal and randomly saw a verse I wrote from years before when working through Beckett's adoption. The verse from Proverbs 3:5 read: "Trust in the Lord with all your heart and lean not on your own understanding." Trust again? I felt infuriated with God and my lot in life. After my own internal storms, I prayed and told God that I'd try — that's all I could really do in my stormy life.

As we waited for our second round of appointments for Gavin, we wanted time to pass quickly. We also waited for the eight-week court date to arrive, which would make Gavin legally ours. Until the termination of parental rights (TPR) took place in our local court, Gavin was not legally our child and could be taken away at any time, a thought that crippled my mind. His birth parents and extended family came to visit quite often, which made us nervous that they were not going to follow through with the adoption plan. Until Gavin's court TPR happened, the birth family could come anytime they wanted to, and it was our legal obligation to allow them to. While they were respectful of our busy schedule, they did come over while our house was up for sale. They also had the right to say what could or could not happen medically. We needed their approval for every medical test or procedure. At this point, we did not know them well, and I worried if they were plotting to keep Gavin and not sign off on the adoption papers. Overall, these red flags warned us that Gavin might not become our son, and I couldn't breathe well until he was.

Waiting, waiting, waiting. We waited on God, on builders, on buyers to purchase our house, on the court system, on doctors and on test results. When would all the waiting end? One night as I went to bed and prayed about wanting things to start going our way, God spoke to my heart and said, "Trust me." God did not reveal how things would turn out. Of course, I wanted answers, but received none. I turned to my Bible and randomly opened to this verse from James 1:2-4: "Consider it pure joy, my brothers, whenever you face trials of many kinds because you know that the testing of your faith develops perseverance. Perseverance must finish its work so that you may be mature and complete, not lacking anything." As this timely verse reminded me of my lessons of trust and persistence, a calmness came over me, giving me for the first time a peaceful sleep until my colicky Gavin woke me up with his piercing cry two hours later needing to be changed and fed.

After a draining and mind-numbing eight weeks since his birth, Gavin's birth parents terminated their parental rights in court, making Gavin our son forever. Overjoyed to the point of tears, we still couldn't rejoice too much as we still fought stormy waters with many more tidal waves ahead of us. The time finally came when we went back to the ENT to test his hearing again. He passed! Yay! A week later, we had our pediatric cardiology appointment. As they strapped him down and did ultrasounds to look at his heart, the doctor smiled and said, "This really is a miracle. His hole in his heart healed, and it's perfect." I smiled, knowing that God performed this miracle. Another week later, we went back to the geneticist who redid the ultrasound on his kidney that was malformed. "I am pleasantly surprised that his kidney isn't abnormal anymore."

"What do you mean?"

"I'm not sure how to explain this, but his kidney is completely normal in shape now. I've never seen anything quite like it." In disbelief, the doctor called others to come witness the miracle.

God whispered to me, "See? I told you I have this."

"The only thing left, though, is your genetic results. We will call you in a few weeks once those come in."

I continued to pray and had everyone I knew do so too. We believed that God could fully heal Gavin.

Two weeks later, the familiar number from Gavin's geneticist appeared on my caller ID. "Hi, Christine. This is Sarah from Children's Hospital. We have Gavin's test results."

"Oh good," I said nervously. "How are they?"

"Well, we are going to have to retest some things. It shows that he is a carrier for a rare genetic disease but would only have this disease if he has the other copy of the gene."

"Um, what? I don't quite get what this means," I anxiously said and added, "What are the chances that he has this copy, and if he has the copy, what health risks are there?"

"First, the chances he has this copy are less than ten percent. But, if he has it, it means he has a seizure disorder that will likely kill him by age one."

"What?" I screamed.

"Please don't worry. Chances are still in your favor. So, please come in and get the blood work done as soon as possible because the results take six weeks to process."

I hung up the phone and again turned to God, asking, WHY? Why us? Why Gavin? And, waiting again! I couldn't handle it. The next six weeks would be unbearable. As I went to bed that night, God came to me in a dream. "Look at what has healed with Gavin already. That's not by accident. Trust me."

Again, God didn't tell me the future. He wanted me to trust Him in that present moment — that moment when I could hardly think straight or even imagine Gavin dying within the year. That news flash boggled my mind, and I could have easily slipped into the pity me mode, but I tried my hardest to take each minute, each hour, and each day at a time. As each day passed, I'd be closer to finding out the truth of Gavin's condition. What exactly were we waiting for this time? The critical news of whether Gavin would have a life or a death sentence. I couldn't fathom losing him now.

With the ups and downs of waiting and being exhausted from so many sleepless nights, we tried our hardest to embrace each moment with Gavin. Beckett adored and bonded quickly with his little brother. He beamed with pride. As Beckett shared his toys, and books, and kissed him good night, we felt joy that only the love of family can bring. We were blessed even with the fear over what the future might hold.

As the six-week mark came, I anxiously called the genetic nurse for Gavin's test results. They were not in yet. I called the next day. No answers yet. And the next day too. No answer. What the heck? Why the delay? Didn't they know that I needed to know now! I lay down on my bed and cried uncontrollably. I kept saying to myself that I just needed to know. Again, God said, "Trust me." A few seconds later, I saw the familiar number on my phone.

"Yes? You have the results."

"Good news. He does not have the copy of that gene. I'm

soooo happy for you and your family."

"What does that mean?"

"It means you have a very healthy boy who overcame so much. His hearing came back, his heart and kidneys came back to normal, and he does not have any serious genetic abnormalities that we usually always see with this syndrome. It's a miracle, really. We don't normally see things like this. I can't explain it, but it feels so wonderful to give a positive report like this for once."

"Oh my gosh. I can't believe it. I'm so happy."

"I'm really ecstatic for you guys. As I said before, I don't get to make calls like this very often."

"What about his lower lip?"

"Well, that's not something we can correct. It just means you should encourage him to smile and not cry. His lip will only droop when he cries. Other than that, you have a healthy little boy. Best to you and your family."

Humbled again. I thanked God for the miracle he performed with Gavin's health issues. In the journey to these test results, God taught me again to keep my eyes on Him as I learned a new level of waiting and trusting Him in the present moment.

Chapter 21: God Speaks Through Children

God sends little children to speak and act for him. In their simplicity and naivety, they say and do things that we adults never would, but which can reveal deep truths about the way the world should be, if we only would have ears to hear and eyes to see.
—Phil Steer

Everyone knows the famous cliché of life — to seize the day because life is short. But it's easy to get caught up in the routines of life, and live thinking we really have all the time in the world — even when we know better. I should know better, especially after Smiley Dan's death many years ago, but I too became immune to the cliché I knew was true.

Life reminded me again just how short it is. My Uncle Emil last came to visit my family in the summer of 2015. Conversations with Uncle Emil always fascinated me as he would share stories of his times working as a rocket scientist at NASA for most of his career. In my uncle's college years, he wrote a master's thesis describing people taking rockets to the moon. These ideas, of course, were before such things were even possible. Professors would shake their heads and wonder how he came up with such dreams for the future. They thought my uncle was strange, yet his ideas were so amazing that people just could not wrap their heads around them. Emil's siblings also thought he was unique when they watched him create different concoctions and blow things up in the family barn.

Years later, though, Uncle Emil helped astronauts go to the moon and proved that his ideas were not so crazy after all. In fact, he was the lead mathematician in the early 1970's who figured out the magic triangle in space with Apollo 11, 12, and 13 to bring the astronauts safely back from space when things went awry. President Nixon honored him with a special plaque, and his legacy lives on through oral history recordings at NASA, as well as many television interviews, including one done by *20/20*. Neil Armstrong is quoted saying that NASA would not be what it is today without Emil, and Armstrong owes much of the success of the mission getting to the moon and back to my uncle. In working at NASA, Uncle Emil invented and published his own mathematical formulas to help the space missions. In my mind, Uncle Emil was another Albert Einstein.

What struck me repeatedly was how someone so intelligent and accomplished often complained that he wasn't that bright, that he didn't do anything that anyone else couldn't do. He said his math was common sense and then wondered why current day astronauts and rocket scientists couldn't figure out how to do things correctly. He would shake his head in disgust. When he complained of this and didn't realize his own talent, I felt God whisper, saying, "See, people who have talent don't always realize their gifts."

God's whisper made me think but didn't make me start writing. Uncle Emil started a novel about the history of space and his observations about NASA and space exploration. Over the last decade, we discussed the frustrations of writing. In one conversation, he told me, "I have so much material, how do I organize it? There's so much in my head that just needs to come out, but it gets lost when I try to write it."

"Well, you just write and then piece it together later after you get it all out," I explained. "It will be chaotic, but it will all come together eventually."

"So, just keep writing?"

"Yep, that's what Grandma told me to do just before she died."

"Hmmm," with a little laugh. "Okay. I will keep trying," Uncle Emil assured me with a warm smile.

Over the years, we asked each other how our books were going, and the perfectionism of writing overcame both of us like a tidal wave. We had lots of ideas but didn't know how to write them clearly so that others would understand. Our usual excuse with procrastination was that we were in our "thinking modes".

It had been some time since I wrote to or talked to Uncle Emil — summer of 2015 when Beckett, my five-year old, came out to greet him in his astronaut costume. We were all so proud to have a future astronaut on our hands. I planned on sharing with Emil this coming summer that I was truly writing this time — not just pretending to — and not just thinking about starting. I also wanted to see him make more progress on his important book that no one else could do justice to.

But then the phone call came, the one you cannot imagine

getting. "Your Uncle Emil passed away," my husband sadly told me while I was at work, teaching. My heart sunk. Feeling as if someone just stabbed my heart, it felt like more than an uncle passed away but also a national hero. In addition, gone was the family historian, as he was the oldest of five kids on my mom's side who knew all the relatives and their stories. Knowing his book did not make publication saddened me. It was a gut wrenchingly blatant and startling reminder for me to keep writing because I don't know when my last days will be. None of us know.

Uncle Emil's death made me melancholy and uncomfortable for other reasons, however. Uncle Emil grew up a Christian, married in the Catholic church, but for reasons unknown to me, he stopped celebrating Christmas some years ago and once made a comment that he didn't really believe in Jesus anymore. It never made sense, but none of us challenged him on this as we didn't feel it was our business to tell him what to think or believe. I'm not one of those holier than thou Christians who will force my beliefs on others. The seeds of a Christian faith were planted a long time ago for Emil, and it was everyone's hope that they'd blossom once again.

Later that evening, after letting the shock of Uncle Emil's death settle in a bit, Beckett, who was five years old at the time, said to me, "Mommy, you need to know that my friend Emil died today."

"I know. Did Daddy tell you that?"

"Yeah, he mentioned it. But Jesus told me first."

"What? What else did Jesus say?" I asked, not knowing what to think.

"He said my friend Emil, the rocket man, died and that he is okay and in heaven with him," Beckett replied matter-of-factly.

"Huh? You mean Daddy told you that?"

"No, Mommy. First, Jesus talked to me. I just said that already. Aren't you listening? Then Daddy said it, and now you and me are talking about Uncle Emil."

"Does Jesus talk to you a lot?"

"Um, yeah. He says things when I pray sometimes."

As I heard Beckett's response, goose bumps permeated throughout my body. I questioned whether I could believe him. While Beckett had a good imagination, most of what he said was fairly accurate. God then whispered to me, saying, "Do you think I only talk to you? It's a lot easier to talk to children because they are more open to hearing me when I speak."

I laughed and remembered the Bible verse about having faith like a child. As a tear dripped from my face, I realized there was no way Beckett knew about my worry of whether Uncle Emil was in heaven or not. The fact that God shared with Beckett that Emil was in heaven was a miraculous gift of knowledge and comfort for the family as we mourned a momentous loss.

PART VI: God's Promptings Toward Our Purpose

Early on in my life, signs appeared that I was meant to be both a writer and teacher, but had it not been for others who showed up and mentored me along the way, my being a teacher for decades as well as writing this book would never have happened. When we are truly meant to do something, God will put people in our lives to help us accomplish His goals that will in turn glorify Him. It's almost unbelievable how these people will be ones we've often felt we've known for a lifetime, like two magnets coming together. In some instances, the connection with these mentors was so automatic that in my heart, I knew they were God-sent.

Chapter 22: Perfect Timing God Sends Mentors

One of the greatest values of mentors is the ability to see ahead what others cannot see and to help them navigate a course to their destination.
—John C. Maxwell

Looking back at my life, it is apparent God tried to talk to me, but my metaphorical "do not disturb" sign was up much of the time. With this door closed, God's knocks could not be heard, due to my own internal frustration, hurt, pain, or life's busy moments. Instead, God spoke to me indirectly through various mentors who would come along at just the perfect time. It may have appeared as a coincidence at first glance, but then upon further reflection, it's obvious God had a hand in it. God used other people at some of the most important crossroads of my life: planting the seeds in my becoming a teacher, helping me become a mother, and even in encouraging me to write this book.

When I was in first grade, I didn't care for school very much. At the Catholic grade school I attended, the teachers made us recite prayers without explaining their meaning, sing songs, which included being thankful for all the hairs on my head, and read silly Dick and Jane books about Spot the dog to whom I couldn't relate. Bored out of my mind, I often daydreamed of different stories I could write. I always enjoyed journaling and writing stories of my own creation, especially about aliens and outer space but didn't think I was very good, especially after overhearing my first-grade teacher at parent/teacher conferences. An older and strict lady said to my parents, "Christine does average work, has average ability, and doesn't show much aptitude on standardized tests. I don't think you should expect her to be any more than a C student." I heard my parents debate her on that, but it didn't matter. The damage was done. As a teacher, I assumed that she earned the right to be an authority figure, and those comments stuck with me until an amazing college professor, years later, challenged my perception of myself. Little did my first-grade teacher know that, when doing standardized tests, I just filled in bubbles because I hated the content of the stories we had to read; I didn't care. And I didn't know that her judgment of me on those tests would affect my self-esteem for most of my school career.

Even though I didn't think much of myself as a student, I still found enjoyment in writing. While in the third grade, my dad gave me glimmers of hope after reading a creative story that I wrote for school. "Christine," he said, "your story about UFO's and aliens is really good. I didn't know you could write like that. You should keep it up. Never know. You might be able to publish your writing someday if you keep working hard."

I didn't think too much of that compliment because it was my dad, not a teacher, saying I was a good writer, but something about being published attracted me. At eight years old, I thought it would be cool to give a published piece of writing to the teacher who said I was just average. From that day on, I started my journals and wrote regularly about life's ups and downs. At the age of eight, I created my own New Year's Eve tradition where I would write down the major events of the year, as well as a list of what I was grateful for. Doing this helped me look back on my life's patterns, as well as how God carried me through different storms in life, allowing me to see blessings along the way. My dad's words said at just the right time planted seeds that laid the foundation for my wanting to become a writer, regardless of my "averageness".

My grades through most of my younger years were just C's and B's. That's what those in power expected, and so I delivered on that average expectation. When I entered the eighth grade, however, an English teacher, Mrs. Langden, took notice of my writing ability. "Why are you in low level, average reading and writing?"

"Because I have just average ability."

"No, you don't. You are better than most of the honors students and don't belong in the blue bird group. From now on, you'll be a red bird." Then Mrs. Langden let me in on a secret, saying, "I know this sounds strange, but God told me that you were in the wrong group, so I have to trust that I'm making the right decision."

Floored. I thought Mrs. Langden was delusional, not only because she decided to move me to an honors class, but also because God spoke to her. Even though I attended a parochial school and she taught religion too, I never heard of God talking to people before. I didn't mind going to the red bird group, though, even if blue was my favorite color. I decided I'd play along with this charade as I could be in the same group as my best friend Amy.

Unbelievably, in high school, I overcame my "average-ness" and earned mostly straight A's, but it was solely because I thought I tricked them all. Somehow, I knew that if I could start out strong by writing a few good papers and do well on quizzes and tests, I could be falsely labeled as "smart" instead of "average." If I could do that, then I could breeze through high school with a new label, unlike grade school. I never believed that I could write well or that I was intelligent. It was a facade, and people believed it, so it worked for me.

Luckily, I tricked everyone enough to earn a spot at the University of Wisconsin-Madison. There, I earned straight A's in my major, and I couldn't believe that just an average ability student could outsmart the brightest. In taking a writing class, one of my professors challenged me, saying, "Christine, you need to read this book, *Lives on the Boundary* by Michael Rose, and see yourself in it. You need to figure out why you don't believe you are intelligent, as well as why you don't see yourself as a writer. If you are going to be a teacher someday, you need to understand this lesson."

Professor Greene wouldn't tell me what the lesson was or how I connected to Michael Rose's story, but as I read on, it became clear. When teachers label students like I was in first grade and that label sticks through grade school, a student's self-esteem could be greatly affected. After years of being in the fog, a light shone. Oh my gosh —I was not dumb, average, or lucky! I was an intelligent, hard-working student who never tricked teachers or professors into giving me A's. This might sound silly that I actually believed I was lucky or tricked them, but having this awakening was a turning point for me, a light that showed me a new path. That meant that I, as a teacher, could help change labeled students' lives by giving them confidence in their abilities. It meant that I could have a real purpose for wanting to teach. And it meant that maybe, just maybe, I was a writer who could one day write a book that could get published and help others.

The idea for this book was spoken to me by God when I

was at church several years ago in 2001. From that time on, I knew I had to journal and track just how God talked to me. Fast forward to 2016, when signs appeared that the time finally came to put these ideas into book form. In 2015, my frugal mother, who never handed out money, approached me to say that she wanted to give me $200 a week to help put my children in daycare, so that not only the kids could keep their skills up over the summer, but so that I could work on writing the book that she felt needed to get done. What? My mom explained, saying that she just felt that God told her that this is what I needed to be doing. Later that same day, my husband asked me when I was going to start getting serious about writing again.

"Have you been talking to my mother?"

"No, why?"

"Well, she said the same thing."

"Weird. I just feel that God wants you to be working on this, and that there is someone out there who needs to read this story that you haven't finished writing yet."

Later that same day, my church asked for volunteers to start a ministry to help those who were angry with God when their prayers were not answered. In explaining to one of the pastors what to say and not say to people who were going through trying times and felt their prayers were ignored, I realized that I just needed to give him my book to explain how God speaks, but it wasn't even half-written yet.

Three signs. God spoke to me through the synchronicity of events. It was obvious. I needed to start writing, and so that night with newfound enthusiasm, I did.

I consistently wrote that whole summer, making myself proud that I could find meaning through words in some of the things that I experienced. At one point, my friend Jill, whom I will discuss more later, knew I was writing, so she gave me a business card of a place that had workshops for writers led by a lady named Karen. Jill said I should take a class there or hire a writing coach.

"I don't want to spend any money on this writing until I have it done to the best of my ability. Spending money on it would be pointless right now," I said, sure of my conviction. "But thanks anyway," I added.

"Okay, but maybe hold onto that business card or look into that place. Think of it for later when you're further along. I found that card at a coffee shop and another writer told me that the writing

help she received from Karen helped her to publish her book."
I carefully tucked the card in my wallet for possible
future use and forgot about it. As a new school year quickly
approached, my writing went into hibernation. If you know
anything about teaching, teachers — most of them — go a
little insane at the start of a new school year. In the craziness
of another new season underway, I began to believe that my
book would never get written. I challenged God, saying,
"God, if you really want this book to happen, you are going to
need to open up the door and send me people who will read
and criticize my work — people who will get the spiritual side
of this, and not people who just nod and say, 'This is good.'"

God didn't answer. Months whizzed by, and like
clockwork every fall, my routine consisted of lesson planning,
grading stacks of papers, and maintaining the house full of
fun, yet sometimes crazy chaos with all my family's wants and
needs. I laughed to myself that book writing really wasn't
meant to be, even though I thought I had a few good ideas that
could help a handful of people. I closed the writing door and
stubbornly wouldn't open it until God provided what I
needed.

My son Beckett started swim lessons that same
summer at the local YMCA. With every lesson, I looked
forward to going so that I could talk to a new friend, Erin — a
kind, down to earth, vivacious lady who listened like I was the
only person in the room who mattered. I don't normally strike
up conversations with strangers, but one afternoon, Erin saw
that I had a copy of Harper Lee's book, *Go Set A Watchman,*
and asked me what I thought of it. That opened a floodgate of
a very fun, intellectual conversation about novels, movies, and
life. The thirty-minute lesson flew by. Over a period of weeks,
we discussed not only novels and movies, but teaching, our
kids who were both adopted, our process in adopting children,
our neighborhoods and friends, our favorite restaurants. A dull
moment with her did not exist, and from random summer
swim lessons, a new friendship blossomed. Through Erin, I
met other book-loving friends who played an instrumental
role in motivating me to write this book.

I challenged God to bring me people who could help
me create the book He wanted and asked me to write. Some of

these new friends were also writing books of their own. One day, Linda wrote me, asking, "Hey, let's exchange writing and give each other feedback. It will help us stay accountable. What do you think? Let me know some dates you are free." Oh no. Things just got real! My heart beat a thousand miles per minute. I knew that I asked God to send me these people, and I knew they were the ones because I had that deja vu feeling that I knew them, but I found it difficult to believe that He'd deliver so quickly. As I thought on it, I really didn't want to commit to writing this book as doing so scared me and made me vulnerable. Part of me still believed I wasn't a real writer. I felt like a phony. But after reading my work, Linda wrote me a quick note, saying, "I see now that my role is not going to be helping you with your writing, so much as it will be to encourage you to keep writing and get this done. You are talented. Keep going!"

My heart and soul beamed with joy at the sincere compliment, and I began to realize that God knew what He was doing all along. The fact that Linda's comments were not my dad's or my husband's or some close friend's made me believe that perhaps I was a writer. God purposefully sent these people to give me the confidence boost I needed to keep me writing and start believing.

This special little writing group lasted only a year, due to new seasons of priorities in people's lives. Even though I understood how their priorities and commitments needed to change, I felt alone again. Who would come along and help me get this book out there? I pleaded with God again that I needed someone who could not only write, but also someone who would understand the spiritual aspects of this memoir. Two years went by. The nudges from God to work on this book never stopped, but I did. I started to give up on my dream of writing, thinking it was only a dream.

Around this two-year mark of not writing, I watched Mercy Me's movie, *I Can Only Imagine.* I couldn't help but be inspired how God worked in the main character, Bart Millard to forgive his father for his life of both physical and emotional abuse. He then started to write his songs authentically from his heart. The songwriter and singer felt that he could never get his song in the hands of the recording artists, but then God worked his magic like He does with perfect timing. Long story short, Amy Grant, another famous Christian singer, decided to have Bart Millard sing his own song about his father who just died, and from there, the rest is history. The song, "I Can Only Imagine," went on to be a runaway hit and GMA song of the year. As I watched this songwriter's story, I heard God say, "See, Christine, I can do anything. Trust me."

I replied in my head, saying, "I do trust you, but without a writing partner, this book won't happen. I can't do it alone."

After saying that prayer to myself, I went to Facebook to see what my "friends" were up to. A post from Becca, more of a close friend of a friend, caught my attention. "Nothing like getting great feedback from your writing workshop group. Spending time with these writers was so self-affirming." I quickly private-messaged Becca, asking for more details. What was she writing? Where did she find a writing workshop? A few seconds later, she wrote back, "Hi. Yes, I'm writing stories about my son's autism. I'm working with Karen and other writers near that local coffee shop in town that you like. It's a great place with supportive people there. You should check it out."

"Thanks, Becca. I'm not quite ready yet, but I'll keep it in mind. Hope you're doing well," I wrote back and thought of how I heard of that place before. I looked through the stack of business cards on my desk and saw that my friend from a few years ago gave me a business card for this place. Might be a sign to go there, but I didn't want to invest financially in this endeavor yet.

Only a week later, after my petition to God for help, I was at a birthday party for my son when I met another mom named Mandy. Mandy was a tall thin blonde whose smile radiated and whose warmth seemed sincere. As we introduced ourselves and realized that our sons often talked fondly about one another, she asked, "Are you a stay-at-home mom, or do you work?"

"I teach high school English, but am off during breaks and summer, so please let me know if you'd ever want a play date!"

"Oh, for sure. English, huh. Do you ever write on your own?" Mandy asked, interested.

"Well, I do, actually, but haven't been writing in the past couple of years because I need to find a real editor or someone to help me take my book to the next level."

"Really? I'm writing a book too. My background is in journalism, but I am a stay-at-home mom right now. What's your book about?" Mandy asked excitedly.

"Um. It is a spiritual memoir of stories and things I've been through and how God gave me signs along the way, how there are no coincidences. I know that sounds strange," I said nervously.

"Oh my gosh. That's awesome and not strange at all. My book is spiritual too."

"What's yours about?"

"My son died at the age of two from a bacterial infection that we did not know he had, and I'm writing about how he gives me signs that he's okay and still around. Those who pass whom we love are still with us."

"I'm so sorry to hear about your son. I can only imagine how hard that is," I said, heartbroken for her. I completely agreed with her — those we love who pass are with us.

"Thank you. Can we exchange phone numbers and email? Maybe we can share our writing with each other. Sounds like we have some things in common," Mandy said with an aura that glowed bright yellow. For going through such dark times four years ago when she lost her son, she definitely had a strength about her.

The minute she shared her story, I knew that God just orchestrated our meeting each other and that my prayer was answered again, just not on my timeline. Mandy and I read each other's books, giving feedback. But then as life became busy at different seasons for both of us, our meetings to discuss our writing became less frequent. Again, I asked God, "Who now? Where do I go with this?" I didn't have to wait long this time for God's answer. The very next day, I received an email at work, asking if I'd like to have a published author speak about her journey of writing and publishing.

I jumped at the chance to call Barb back and learned that she was on the committee to connect area authors with schools. While I was interested in Barb having an author meet my students, I really wanted to talk to her about writing and publishing for my own knowledge. I met with her several times over the summer to discuss her writing journey. Barb's book *Paddle For a Purpose* fascinated me — she and her husband paddled the kayak they built from Minnesota to the Gulf of Mexico to do service along the way. I felt an instant connection to Barb because her trip was a response to a whisper from God. As we met every few weeks and I gave Barb feedback on some of her poetry, she gave me the best gift of all — a true interest in my writing. A strong Christian herself who believed and understood the themes of my book, she gave me insightful feedback. Her wisdom and guidance were just what I needed to keep going on my journey.

Months later, right before Black Friday, Barb wrote, saying, "Christine, as you know, I worked with Karen at that place in town. Her coaching, editing, as well as all the people I met in her classes, helped me get my book published. She has a special for Black Friday. Here is a screenshot of her website. Check it out."

I can be stubborn at times, but I couldn't ignore this sign even if my frugal side wanted to wait. As I shared this information and price-tag with Phil, he supportively said, "What are you waiting for? Don't worry about the price right now. You'll make it up when you sell this book. You are meant to go there. You've been told three different times in three different ways. I don't think God can make it any clearer, and I don't want Him to do any more to get our attention."

"Are you sure? You're going to have to entertain the kids while I work on this!"

"Yes. Just sign up with that Karen lady. Get it done. God wants this book out there," Phil insisted. I called Karen right away, figured out how to use PayPal, and sent her the first twenty pages of my book with a meeting date three days later. It really was happening. What did I just start?

As Monday arrived, I felt jittery and vulnerable all day. Would Karen, my new writing coach, like my writing? Would it be good enough to be considered something worthy of publishing? As I first walked into her studio, I was greeted by a large rectangular table with a library of books, including those of all the students whom she helped publish. Inspirational art and writing quotes also decorated the warm, burgundy-colored room. Waiting for Karen to walk down the stairs to start our meeting felt like being back in high school, anxious to see what grade Mrs. Cantwell gave me on a paper. Did I please the teacher, and if I didn't, did it even matter? I thought that it didn't because God would help this get published if it was meant to be, yet it would be good confirmation if a "real writer" said it was something worth pursuing.

Karen complimented my writing and her belief in my work. I breathed a sigh of relief. This served as another catalyst for my motivation to revise and finish this project. The writing and publishing of this book not only took God's perfect timing but also my finally listening to Him as well as to the people He sent my way to help me put the pieces in motion.

Chapter 23: God's Timing in Finding a Job

God's voice thunders in marvelous ways; he does great things beyond our understanding. He says to the snow, 'Fall on earth' and to the rain shower, 'be a mighty downpour' (Job 37:5-6). Basically, he's saying, just do the thing I've created you to do. You are the rain, so rain. You are the snow, so snow. God is asking you to be the thing he's already created you to be.

—*Shauna Niequist*

After the constant decade-long struggle to have a child passed, I turned my attention to finding a new teaching job. The year after Beckett was born, Emerson High School had a job opening. At that time, I taught in a suburban city, a forty-minute drive away — much too long for me. I really wanted to apply to Emerson High School as it would be a much closer commute in a family-oriented small town that had a reputation as one of the best school districts, not only in the state of Wisconsin, but within the nation. However, as much as I wanted to apply, Beckett just turned one year old, and I already had my hat in the ring for adoption number two. While the Emerson High School job felt like the perfect one, I didn't really want to be at a new job and have to take time off once the second adoption came along. Sadly, I did not apply for this dream job. As perfect as it was, it screamed wrong timing. I trusted my gut and decided to wait and hope that something this appealing would come my way again.

Fast forward a few years. Gavin was born in May of 2013. That summer, the town I lived in and the high school I graduated from had an English position open up. I applied to be closer to home and had a final interview as one of two remaining candidates. Unfortunately, I ended up not getting that job, and for a while, my ego was crushed. It seemed like the perfect fit, and I didn't understand why I wasn't offered the job, but over time, I decided to focus on the good and what I did have (a loving family, good health, and a job where I loved teaching my students). After getting over my bruised ego, I realized that not getting that job was just meant to be for whatever reason. Again, I had to be okay not knowing all the whys in life, a lesson that I often needed to relearn.

A few weeks later, another town close by posted a teaching position. I applied and made it to the final round again. When offered the final interview, I felt God whisper to me, "Wait. Don't take that job. It's not the right timing or the right one." Really God? God knew how frustrated I was and that I desired to relocate for a shorter commute. It was hard to trust what I heard; I didn't want to pass this job up. What if nothing else came my way? When I turned down the final interview, the principal replied, "That's too bad because we were really interested in you and thought you could help our district out with your experience." After hearing that, I sure hoped that I heard God correctly. Nothing else opened up that year, and so I made the best of the situation, going back to my 40-minute commute and enjoying my students. I couldn't help but think there had to be some student or student(s) whose path I was meant to cross.

When Gavin was born that year, my past principal became demanding and ignored the fact that I was on maternity leave. He emailed, asking me to come back to work to give a student who was failing my class (and when I say failing — I mean he had a 15 percent; 60 percent is passing) another chance at passing the final exam. My principal forgot how I was on maternity leave with a newborn who happened to be a week old and who had many critical health issues. I politely explained that I disagreed with his decision to give the student a re-test, but that if he wanted to do so, someone else would have to do it as I was on family medical leave; I offered an alternative, saying I could help regrade it when I came back the next school year. He wrote back, saying, "I'm not sure why you need a leave of absence. You didn't give birth and just adopted a baby." When I first saw his email, I thought it would be congratulatory, yet it was only a demand for me to come back to work before the law legally required.

When I came back to work that fall after my leave of absence, I found out that I wasn't considered for a raise like many other teachers received. The principal commented that I "slowed down since having kids." All my years of experience didn't matter anymore. He only had to judge me on that past year, ignoring decades of excellent teaching and leadership at that school.

Feeling as if a great injustice occurred, I cried during my commute home. That night, as tears poured out like a faucet, I regretted not following through with the job the year before or even the other school three years prior. That's when I heard God whisper, "Check online. Look at the online teaching openings." It was only February, though, a month when teaching jobs usually weren't even posted for the following year yet. Again, the voice debated with me, saying to "Just go check." Like a little child finally obeying her father, I checked the computer to see what teaching jobs might be available for the coming year.

As I read across the openings, holy cow, there it was — Emerson High School — the school I wanted to apply to years ago. Glancing over the application information, I found out that very night was the last day to apply. Yikes! I had to get busy immediately.

Nevertheless, I stayed up past 1 a.m., getting all my materials together. I even boldly took a risk and emailed the Emerson High School (EHS) principal directly, letting him know of my sincere interest. Gracious enough to write back, he thanked me for my interest. More things came into alignment, showing me that going to EHS was meant to be. My past principal, the one before Goliath, actually knew the EHS principal and offered to put in a good word about me by emailing him directly. Later that week, while at a parenting conference at church, I met a past teacher from EHS who told me how difficult obtaining a job there would be but that if I did so, I'd love the atmosphere and great leadership. Another week later, a teacher I worked with at my current school attended a conference and met the literacy coach from EHS. Somehow, it came up that I applied there. She reassured him of what a great teacher I was and how I would "be a major loss to the district if I left." What timing for all these signs to align.

After weeks of several interviews, I was offered the job and filled with gratitude as a result.

Reflecting on my career choices for the past few years, I knew that all these happenings were meaningful encounters created by God and the Holy Spirit to tell me that the correct path was laid out in front of me. In looking for the right job, it felt as though my spiritual supporters cheered me on and gave me signs to keep going. If I didn't listen or have faith early on in God's whispers over which job to pass up or which job to apply for and take, I might have missed my opportunity. God orchestrated all these signs through His nudges that kept coming up until I listened.

PART VII: God Provides Insight on Physical and Mental Health

People often look to doctors to heal their loved ones, but in the end, God is the ultimate healer and is all knowing in what is wrong, both physically and mentally. Sometimes, He will guide people to help them figure out what is wrong or put certain situations in our lives, so that we slow down and listen to Him. Other times, terrible things happen, but God can use these situations for our good to inform and heal as He did in one friendship of mine. The friendship faded, but the lessons healed some deeply rooted beliefs from my past.

Chapter 24: Asking God for Clarity with Pain

*Sometimes I thank God for unanswered prayers. Remember when
you're talking to the guy upstairs that just because he doesn't
answer doesn't mean he doesn't care. Some of God's greatest gifts
are unanswered prayers.*

— *Garth Brooks*

Years later, even when in seasons of joy, the cliches that
people spoke to me when I went through years of waiting on God
still haunted me. Not too long after Beckett was born, I felt God
whisper to get some lab work done. Overall, I felt okay, but
sometimes felt fatigued and nauseous. I wasn't sure if that was due
to being a new mommy or due to something else. It turned out that
my Vitamin D level was too high, and my hormones were off
again. When I shared this information with a friend who happened
to be a nurse, as well as someone I often talked to about God, I
asked her if she ever had any patients with toxic levels of Vitamin
D. She quickly responded that she never heard of such a thing, and
that I just "need to give it to God and trust Him to heal me." That's
all nice in theory, but like others did to me in the past, I felt that
she falsely judged and misunderstood my level of trust in God. As
a result, I became irritated. After all, it was because I trusted God's
whispers that I had the labs done in the first place. I did trust. Why
couldn't people see that? I felt defensive.

After thinking about this comment, I realized that being told
to "trust in God" spiraled me back to the days when I went through
many years of miscarriage. People would tell me to "trust in God"
or that "God has a plan" or even that "God never gives more than a
person can handle". Hmmm, seemed to me that I drowned several
times when I continued to have miscarriages. The truth was that
God did give me more than I could handle, but by leaning on Him,
I somehow survived huge heartaches. But why, years later, was I
so hurt with this phrase?

In reality, my friend's idea about trusting in God was
actually a gift for me to see that my grief was not completely
healed from the past. Grief came in waves, and her words
showed me where I needed healing. That night, I prayed to

God to show me what the source of my anger was with this pain, and in my dreams, the Holy Spirit answered.

For years, people gave me the false impression that if I trusted more, my disappointments with God would end — that God would answer my prayers and give me the baby that I so desperately desired, prayed and longed for. While I became a parent through adoption, I never had a biological child. I foolishly felt I didn't measure up as a woman and that since my child was not from me, I couldn't be a "real" parent.

While God did lead me down the path of many answers in my infertility journey, in truth, the solution was never found. I'll most likely never know why I could not carry a baby to term with endometriosis while many other women could. No amount of faith or action on my part could have changed my fate. I had no control over having a biological child, and I had to learn to be okay with the unknown chaos that that lack of control and lack of definitive answers caused. For someone like me who likes answers and problems solved, this situation proved beyond challenging. People tried to provide solutions and fixes, but in the end, none of them worked and only made me feel more depressed and alone.

By being told over and over to just "trust in God" when I went through a crisis, people minimized my pain and made me feel attacked by questioning my level of faith. While many people shallowly acknowledged my pain, very few really embraced it and felt it with me. I prayed and prayed and prayed for a baby as others did for me too, but that didn't mean that God would answer that prayer in the way that I wanted.

Some Christians even had the gall to say that maybe I did something not pleasing to God and that not having a baby was my punishment. I don't believe that either, as a loving God does not work that way; I was shocked people would even suggest something so crazy. We will not always know why some prayers are answered while others are not. We are not God. We can't know. People telling me to "trust in God" implied my prayers would be answered my way.

A better prayer would have been for me to trust that God would get me through whatever His will would be; that I'd have the strength to know what path to take and when, that my yearning for a biological child be healed if I was never going to have one. Finally accepting that I might never know the answer to why I could not have a biological child freed me from my pain. I didn't like the loss of control, but it took faith to accept that I didn't need to be in control; God already had my back. He had a plan all along, but it wasn't for me to know until God's perfect timing. In the storm, I needed to live in the present moment and rely and trust that things would work out somehow. They always do, though, not always how we'd like.

And so with my toxic levels of Vitamin D, I realized that trusting God would not equate to necessarily understanding why that happened. All I could do was trust that God would guide me to a doctor who could help figure that out. While my levels evened out as I went off Vitamin D, I never knew why it happened in the first place, but I learned to be content not knowing.

Chapter 25: Ideas God Whispers Through Intuition

To hear the whisper of God, you must turn down the volume of the world. Find time to disconnect from everything around you and be still in His presence today. He is waiting for you to draw near.
— *Anonymous*

After finally finding the love of my life and marrying Phil, I imagined my first year of marriage to be full of joy and excitement — where we'd spend days happily strolling along, hand in hand, talking about life's deepest secrets, as well as our future dreams. We'd build our dream house on a hill by a lake, have two or three children and coach their sports teams — specifically baseball and basketball. These daydreams before married life were not reality.

Instead, I lacked vitality and my vivacious self disappeared. Life was a conveyor belt with constant movement, yet I felt stuck. I found myself thirsty all the time, sometimes with heart palpitations, and a slight depression for no reason at all. As the days and year dragged on at a snail's pace, I carried a cloud of fatigue everywhere I went. I naively concluded that was the result of married life — not the happiest realization, I know. In pictures from that time period, people pointed out how I looked like a ghost and had no real complexion, no matter how much blush I put on. It was odd, but I thought my paleness was some strange phenomena with my makeup. Finally, one morning, my heart started palpitating off its normal rhythm. It hurt with a tingling sensation of feeling shocked as I moved, and my brain went on worry overload, wondering if I could be having a heart attack. I considered how heart attacks in women often go undiagnosed. In addition, in those last few months, my bones ached. Something had to be wrong...

"Please, find out what's wrong with me," I said sternly to the Urgent Care doctor.

"Nothing is wrong," Dr. Bug assured me. "You are in perfectly good health, and you're only thirty years old."

"No, really, I'm not making these symptoms up."

"Are you sure you are not stressed out or going through some anxiety with work? A racing heartbeat can be a sign of anxiety."

"I'm always stressed out and never get symptoms like this." And then, right when I thought there was no hope in finding out what was wrong, God whispered to me, "Demand a blood test."

"Why?" I asked God in my mind.

"Don't ask why. Just trust me. Something will show up," God said in my heart.

As the doctor started to leave, I mustered up the words and said, "We need to do a blood test."

"Well, I don't think it is necessary, but if it will make you feel better, I will order one for you," Dr. Bug replied.

"Thanks, and please let me know the results as soon as you get them."

Dr. Bug half-heartedly nodded with a smile that said he thought I was nuts.

Two days later, Dr. Bug called to say that he wanted to recheck my calcium levels as they were a bit high. He acted like this was no big deal and probably a lab error. Since the Internet didn't have much information on this, I didn't have WebMD's advice to worry over.

As planned, I had my calcium levels rechecked a few weeks later. Within a few hours, the caller ID showed the clinic's phone number. Uh-oh. That's a pretty quick reply, I thought. Wonder what they found. Dr. Bug called saying, "Christine — I'm glad you insisted on that blood test. On the second draw, your calcium levels are higher than normal again. This may mean your parathyroid is off."

"My what? What's a parathyroid?" I asked, concerned.

"It regulates the calcium in your body, and if it's off, you can get strange symptoms. I want you to see an endocrinologist who will figure out if you need to have one of the four parathyroids removed. One of them may have a tumor on it, which would cause it not to function correctly," Dr. Bug said.

It turns out that I needed a rare surgery to remove one of my parathyroids that did indeed have a tumor on it. The out of whack parathyroid made my calcium levels dangerously high, which caused my previous symptoms of fatigue, thirst, heart palpitations, etc... The minute the parathyroid was removed, all my symptoms went away much like a magician waving his wand.

As I sat up in the hospital recovery room, my throat ached from the endotracheal tube that had been used during the surgery, but with the parathyroid removed, I surprisingly found myself full of energy and life. My ghost-like complexion now radiated with natural color. As I came back from the dead, I realized how God led me to find the solution to my strange symptoms when He told me to demand that blood test from Dr. Bug. Through this instance, God taught me that He helped me in my time of need, and that hearing God happened when I was open to listening to Him.

Chapter 26: God Comes to the Rescue

Where you are today is no accident. God is using the situation you are in right now to shape you for the place He wants to bring you into tomorrow. Trust Him.

— Anonymous

While God desires constant communication with us, sometimes life brings situations where God will not only talk, but nag and yell to get our attention in order for us to follow through on His will. This nagging from God happened to me in a few critical situations that, had I not listened, life might have taken an unexpected turn for the worse.

My father-in-law complained of some shooting pain in his chest that would come and go. When he missed the family graduation party two hours away due to pain and fatigue, I questioned my mother-in-law, "Isn't he supposed to have his hip replacement surgery in a few weeks? How long has he had this heart pain?"

"He's had this pain before. It's no big deal," she said matter-of-factly.

But knowing how he hated to miss family gatherings, my intuition fired up, and I knew there had to be more going on.

"He should not be going to have a hip surgery until doctors check over his heart pain, especially since there is a family history of stroke and heart attacks." I'm not a nurse, but this just seemed to be common sense. Why wasn't it to my mother-in-law and the rest of Phil's family, especially since some of them have careers in nursing?

Despite trying to convince my mother-in-law to get him checked out before surgery, she replied, "No, he'll be fine." Her old school German stubbornness did not help the situation.

I shared my concerns with my husband that night who downplayed the issue as well. "They are grown-ups. They can make their own decisions. Just let them be. My mom is a nurse and would know what to do if it were serious."

Frustrated that no one listened or took my thoughts seriously, I slept on it. That night, God came to me in a dream as He often did when He really needed me to listen. God said in my heart, "Don't give up. You need to convince Phil." God didn't tell me how to convince everyone or even why I needed to, but somehow, I knew I had to quickly put my persuasive hat on.

The next morning, the ideas just flowed out of me as I spoke to Phil about my dream. "Phil, remember all the other times I've had dreams or had nudges from God that changed the course of our lives? You know when God talks to me that it is for real and that we can trust Him. In the past, God told me to get my parathyroid checked out by demanding a blood test. He told me to apply for a new teaching job when I needed a closer commute. He led us to adopt our kids. God is basically yelling at me to make sure that you convince your family that your dad gets his heart pain checked out before he has his hip surgery. You must help make this happen!"

"Okay, okay. I'll talk to my sister and get her thoughts on it. If we convince her, you know that Mom and Dad will listen. " Oh great. His sister, Denise, is also a nurse. Will she brush it off too?

Thankfully, Phil convinced his sister to discuss this matter with his parents. A few days later, his dad had a series of tests. The cardiologist told him he had major blockage, which required heart surgery that week. The doctors explained that if he went through with his hip surgery first before fixing his heart, he may not have lived through it. Luckily, he made it through his surgery with flying colors and a year later, had a successful hip replacement.

Similar to God getting my attention to help my father-in-law, God also brought people to mind so I could reach out to them. For days, God kept reminding me of Mrs. Cantwell, my past high school English teacher. It had been a few years since we got together for lunch. I owed all the credit and blame to her for my becoming an English teacher. Over the years, she and I stayed in touch. She was there for my wedding and served as not only a mentor, but also a wise friend who cheered me on and cried with me throughout life's ups and downs.

In a random dream, God said to me, "You need to call Mrs. Cantwell. She's getting older now and won't live forever. You should give her a draft of your book for her feedback."

I thought that was a great idea, but I didn't listen. Life kept me busy with the kids and with work, so I said I'd follow through in a few months when things slowed down.

God didn't like that answer, however. Every day, her name

came to mind with this overwhelming feeling that I had to call her. I kept thinking, though, that I wanted to give more time to getting my book perfect before I'd share it with her.

Again, God didn't like that answer. Every time I gave a reasonable excuse, Mrs. Cantwell's name kept coming to mind. This went on for three solid weeks. "Fine. I'll call later today once the kids go to bed," I said to God's nagging voice in my head.

The magical time on a Saturday afternoon finally arrived. The children napped. Reluctantly, I dialed Mrs. Cantwell's phone number.

"Hello."

"This is Christine Nekas Thoma." I always used my maiden name too, in case she forgot my married name.

"Oh wow. I was thinking about reaching out to you. I take it you heard what happened to me three weeks ago?"

"No, what?"

"Oh, c'mon. You must have heard from one of the other teachers? Everyone seems to know because I told one person at St. Vinny's where I volunteer. That guy told a retired teacher, and all those people talk, so now the whole world knows."

"No, honestly. I have no idea what you're talking about. For three weeks, it's been on my mind to call you and ask you to get together, and that's why I'm finally calling."

"What timing! Well, three weeks ago, I had both a stroke and a heart attack. I was in the ICU for four days. I'm doing better now, but it really scared me. I still have physical therapy I need to go to."

"Oh my gosh, I can't believe it. I'm so glad you are okay. It was three weeks ago that God told me to call you."

"Really? Well, you've always had intuition like that. What else did God tell you?"

"Let's get together, and I'll explain."

We made plans and met for lunch a few days later. When I first saw her at our local diner, I felt relieved that after just three weeks of going through one of the scariest health crises of her life she lit up with joy and calm demeanor. While she looked tired, she still had a twinkle in her grey-blue eyes, and mentally, seemed as sharp as ever with her sarcastic wit and humor — a relief for sure. After explaining how I worked on my book the past year, she took my rough draft and said she would be delighted to read it and give me some feedback. I felt as if I transported back to high school, nervously waiting to see if my work earned an A.

Now twenty-four years later, we laughed at our first encounter. As she was getting ready to leave, she said, "So is this book any good?"

"I'm not sure, but I know you are supposed to help me with it."

"If you're not saying it's good, that must mean it's pretty special. I think there is definitely a need for what you are trying to say and probably a market for it."

We carried on like that for awhile, and as we gave our hugs goodbye, she looked me in the eye and said she was glad that I called. "At age seventy-seven, you just never know what the next day holds."

And that made me think that at any age, we just don't know. Hearing that motivated me to continue working on the book and the things I'm meant to do in this life.

Because months went by with no call from Mrs. Cantwell, I assumed she either didn't read my book or didn't know how to give me the news that she didn't like it. I called her anyway to catch up. In the middle of our talk, she interrupted our conversation. "Christine, I meant to call you. Remember that book draft you gave me several months ago?"

How could I forget. "Yes," I hesitatingly responded.

"I think you have something there," Mrs. Cantwell replied.

"You mean it's good?" I asked, waiting on her every word.

"Oh, I didn't say that, but I think it's worth doing. There will be lots of people who will like and need your story. Sorry, I didn't make many edits to it. I don't have the stamina I used to, and there weren't a lot of edits to make."

Getting a genuine compliment from Mrs. Cantwell was a rarity. Her feedback was enough to keep me going and give me confidence that the book should be pursued. For whatever reason, my soul yearned for her validation, and she delivered it.

Ch 27: Mama Bear's Mission to Help Her Son

A worried mother does better research than the FBI.
— Anonymous

From the moment Beckett was little, I noticed that he never liked to look me straight in the eye or look at the camera for pictures. I assumed he was just shy. When we'd go to mommy and child classes or try out a new sport, he'd often be the one daydreaming or picking grass on the baseball field. Sometimes, he'd show much hesitation in a new situation, and instead of showing excitement over something fun, he'd hide out by the door, afraid to come in and make new friends. I often wondered if he suffered from some form of social anxiety, but his pediatrician said his behavior was age appropriate and not to worry unless it prevented him from joining in the fun all together. I accepted the fact that Beckett marched to the beat of his own drum and felt that being his own person and not a follower was a trait to embrace rather than change.

In kindergarten and first grade, Beckett did well in school, learning reading and math quickly and scoring in the ninety-some percentile on standardized tests. Toward the end of first grade, though, his scores started to drop, and by second grade, his test scores went to a low eleventh percentile. Thinking that he just didn't care and blew off the tests, I talked to him about taking the test seriously and doing his best, so we knew how to help him. On a retake, his scores came out the same, and Beckett cried, saying he did his best. My heart ached. What happened to my smart child? Was he now just a bad test taker? How could he drop so much? As a teacher researcher myself, I was on a mission to figure this out.

Meanwhile, his teacher, Mrs. Smith, said that he often rubbed his eyes and he complained of headaches. I also noticed that his eyes were often red and watering. They looked uncomfortable. Mrs. Smith said that he had trouble focusing when she taught or when he had to work independently, especially with writing. We tested him for allergies and found that he was allergic to grass, so we made sure to give him some medicine for that. But even with that finding, his schoolwork did not improve, and he often looked around the room with his sore and watery eyes as lessons were taught.

Nothing made sense to me as a parent or as a teacher. In my heart, I knew that Beckett was a deep thinker who could build complex Lego sets and perform at a high level with reading and math. All his teachers before this said he had so much potential. So many questions popped up in my mind, consuming my thoughts and making me want to figure out how to best help him without turning him off to school altogether. So many times, he cried at night as he had to write sentences with vocabulary words or write a paragraph or poem. The frustration that he felt was real, and his reluctance with schoolwork baffled me.

Was he just avoiding schoolwork, especially writing because he is a boy who doesn't care for it? Did he have anxiety and fear of failure and therefore struggled? Had I put too much pressure on him? Did he have an undiagnosed learning disability, especially in the area of writing? Did he have Attention Deficit Hyper-Active Disorder (ADHD) or some other form of it? Did he have a sensory processing disorder? I didn't know the answers but prayed continuously for guidance. I begged God to show me the solution to this mystery.

Beckett's teacher first recommended that we see a child psychologist. It took us five months to get an appointment. When we finally saw Mrs. Dalton, the child psychologist, she wanted Beckett's teacher and us to fill out the standard Connors form to figure out if he had ADHD. According to the results, there was not enough evidence to conclude he had ADHD. If he did, she said he'd have trouble following a four-step process of directions at home, and that it would be obvious to us that there was an issue. Mrs. Dalton concluded, however, that he had slight anxiety and that working with him on a growth mindset and believing in himself would be beneficial. She also suggested that we get evaluated by an Occupational Therapist to rule out a sensory processing disorder.

I went along with that recommendation, but my gut felt that wasn't the right issue. This was new territory for me. What did I know? We saw Ms. Miller, an OT, who said that Beckett had a sensitivity to hearing and some coordination issues. His letter formation needed work, and perhaps relearning the right techniques would help his writing. So he did writing exercises and other strange drills for the next eight weeks. As I asked Ms. Miller what she was looking for or what a particular exercise was meant to do, she had trouble giving me a specific answer. I felt God telling me to stop going there as it wasn't helping anything. Even with that, I didn't know where else to go. I prayed for guidance and felt frustrated with the lack of answers. Around this time, a neuropsychologist that we were on a wait list for called with an appointment for the next day. Watching Beckett be put through six hours of IQ testing was unbearable. Again, it was apparent that Beckett's eyes hurt. The neuropsychologist concluded that he believed Beckett suffered from an inattentive type of ADHD. "And this is why he has trouble writing. He doesn't have the attention needed to organize and think through his thoughts," the neuropsychologist said. He recommended putting him on medication.

My stomach rumbled, and I left that appointment feeling completely distraught. I don't know why, but I didn't trust that doctor's recommendation. That evening as I discussed things with my good friend who happened to be an occupational therapist, she asked, "Why don't you check to see if he has a functional vision problem? I think you need to rule that out," she insisted. My friend brought up that idea several months earlier, and I dismissed it at the time mainly because I never heard of such a thing. That seemed like an unrealistic issue in my mind.

"But he can see 20/20. They check vision at school, and he always passes fine," I said.

"No, you can have a functional vision problem and be able to see 20/20. A functional eye doctor will test depth perception, eye tracking and eye teaming. These skills are not tested during a typical vision screening," she explained.

"Wait, what?"

"Yes, it's true. I'll send you a website and a screening quiz to take," she said.

As I looked at the quiz, Beckett had almost every symptom. Headaches from near work. Check. Words run together when reading. Check. Burning, itchy and watery eyes. A major check. Skips/repeats lines when reading. Check. Difficulty copying from the chalkboard. Check. Omits words when reading. Check. Writes uphill or downhill and overall poor handwriting. Check. Misaligns digits/columns of numbers. Check. Reading comprehension down. Check. Trouble keeping attention on reading and completing assignments. Check. Says I can't before trying. Check. Clumsy, loses things. Check. Forgetful/poor memory. Check. A score of twenty or more indicated a cause for concern. Beckett had a score of over forty. In my head, I heard God say, "Christine, pay attention to this." And for the first time on this journey to figure out what the heck was going on with Beckett, this made sense. Amen! I never heard of someone who could see 20/20 yet have a functional vision problem.

After taking the quiz, I called up the closest eye therapy clinic about thirty minutes away and made an appointment. A few days later, we met Dr. Brandon Begotka for a comprehensive functional vision exam. At this exam, the doctor would assess visual skills such as visual information processing, binocular function, fixation, tracking, accommodation, and eye teaming.

"What symptoms does Beckett have?"

"Well, almost every item on your questionnaire, but mainly eye rubbing, short attention span with schoolwork, poor handwriting and decreasing test scores on reading and math. One neuro-psych doctor thinks he has ADHD, but I'm not feeling that's the right diagnosis," I said, desperately seeking help. "He didn't present the way most of my students do with that diagnosis."

"With a functional vision problem, a person's visual system isn't functioning correctly, so reading and learning become difficult, and performance is affected. Even sports can become difficult. Good vision requires your entire system (eyes, brain visual pathways) to work together. When it doesn't, even a person with 20/20 eyesight can experience difficulty reading, writing, and processing information," Dr. Begotka explained.

"Oh wow. I'm not imagining this then. What about ADHD?"

"Oh, glad you mentioned that. ADHD and a functional vision problem can look very similar. If a person has an untreated functional vision problem and gets a diagnosis of ADHD based on observed signs and symptoms, they may receive a treatment that doesn't actually address the root cause of those signs and symptoms," Dr. Begotka said.

Meanwhile, Dr Begotka examined Beckett. I kept thinking and feeling that this had to be what's wrong. Nothing else made sense. God whispered to me, "Just trust and have faith." As I hoped and prayed we'd get an answer that finally made sense, Dr Begotka said, "Well, Beckett is a classic textbook case of someone who has a functional vision problem. He has issues with saccadic eye movement, eye focusing and accommodation and eye teaming/binocularity."

"What does that mean? Does this all correlate to the issues we are seeing with him and his schoolwork?"

"Oh, for sure. With his eye focusing or accommodation issues, he can have trouble paying attention in school because of headaches, eye rubbing and his eyes become fatigued, all which can make him fidgety. You might see him staring off into space or talking to a nearby student," Dr. Begotka said.

"Yes, his teachers have said that."

"With his eye movement and teaming issues, it can be challenging for him to see a line of text as single and clear when reading. It takes more effort than it should, and he might give up or read at a slower rate. This can also cause him to see double. The eyes must move accurately from word to word. If they don't, he might skip a word or re-read the same word," Dr. Begotka explained.

"Wait. This makes sense. When he was in 5K and 1st grade, the text was bigger, so he could see it, but as his reading levels have increased, the text became smaller. He's probably having trouble seeing it, which is why we are noticing the problem now on test scores too," I said like I discovered the key to the universe.

"Exactly. "

"Does this explain why he sometimes does letter and number reversals too?" I asked.

"Sure does. How does he do in sports?"

"Well, he started avoiding them, and often squints when a ball is thrown to him," I said.

"With therapy, you'll see his eye-hand and eye-body coordination and handwriting improve too. Kids with functional vision problems can even see double in sports."

"Beckett, what did you see when you played baseball?" I asked.

"Well, I'd see two balls."

"What?"

"Yes, seeing double is common," Dr. Begotka said.

"Well, how did you know which ball to catch?"

"I'd guess. If I was wrong, I'd get hit by the ball," Beckett said.

My heart hurt that he didn't know the rest of the world does not see like that. I wish I knew earlier he needed help.

His patient education assistant, Kelly, gave me some goggles to put on, which made me see double. "Now, read this," she said to me.

"I can't. It's too blurry and is giving me a headache," I complained right away.

"That's what your son always sees when he tries to read or catch a ball. The fact that he's done as well as he has thus far shows you how smart he is," Kelly explained.

I knew it. I knew he was smart and that there had to be some explanation for all these symptoms. With tears in my eyes, I felt such grief for what Beckett endured, but I also felt tears of joy for finding what appeared to be the answer to his struggles. "So, how do we fix all this?"

"It will be a lot of work but worth it. He will need to come to our clinic once a week for forty-five minutes for the next nine months of eye therapy, and you will have to work with him for twenty to thirty minutes a day five to six days a week doing eye exercises. The purpose of our office visits is to build his visual skills and keep track of how you are doing with the exercises at home. We have to retrain the eyes and the brain to work together with activities that will help the visual system correctly process information that the brain receives from the eyes."

"What will the exercises entail?"

"We will use a variety of lenses, prisms, 3-D targets, exercises and activities to develop visual skills so that his functional vision system works easily and efficiently."

"What outcomes would you expect at the end of therapy?" I asked.

"Most students after six to nine months will find that learning is easier, that reading levels and speed increase, and time spent on homework is less. Additionally, visual information processing skills like visualization will be developed that are important for math, spelling, reading comprehension and composition."

"Okay. Sign us up. You had me at learning is easier," I said.

With a medical diagnosis from the eye doctor, we had Beckett's elementary school professionals create a 504 Plan with some simple accommodations, mainly asking his teachers to enlarge the text on his handouts so he could read them. Under Section 504 of the Rehabilitation Act, a 504 Plan is a Civil Rights law. Schools create a formal plan that give kids with disabilities the support they need. I could tell the team, which consisted of the school principal, the school psychologist, and his teacher, were skeptical. They never really heard of a functional vision problem before this. I couldn't blame them, though. Having taught so long myself, I never heard of this diagnosis either.

"According to the American Optometric Association, one in four children and twenty percent of the population has a functional vision problem that can go undetected and be misdiagnosed as a learning disability or as ADHD. A functional vision problem affects a person's ability to learn," I explained to the team.

The school psychologist said, "But we do test all the children's vision at school."

"What you screen for is a child's acuity or their ability to see clearly. You don't test their eye teaming, tracking, focusing, or visualization. Beckett has 20/20 acuity but a serious functional vision problem," I stated. The surprised look on the team's faces made me realize they were in shock and didn't know what to think.

It made me so sad to think that more people don't know about this and are going through the same thing. As I read testimonials and did my own research on the diagnosis, I found that there is a high rate of juvenile delinquents who have had an undiagnosed eye function issue. And that broke my heart. They basically went through school not fitting into our culture of sports because their coordination was affected, and they didn't perform well in school because reading and writing became a struggle. After all, eighty percent of sensory input is visual, according to Dr. Brenda Montecalvo in *Visual Secrets for School Success*. As a result, these teens didn't fit in and chose a path of struggle and trouble. God whispered to me as I read some of this research, "You just changed Beckett's path forever and saved him from a negative self-fulfilling prophecy." I'm so glad I trusted God and my gut feeling on this one. I feel compelled to write and tell everyone about this often undiagnosed problem as I'm sure there are many more stories like Beckett's yet to be uncovered.

The eye therapy journey is not for the faint of heart. Watching Beckett diligently do his eye exercises each day sometimes with eye patches, prisms, or other optical filters reminded me of when I needed to do physical therapy for nine months on my knee after having micro-fracture surgery. Similar to needing to build my muscles back through repetitive and sometimes painful exercises, Beckett worked hard to improve his visual skills. Those first six months proved frustrating as we didn't see many changes at all. His focus in school was still off. He still skipped words when reading, and his test scores remained low. At times, I'd question God and the eye doctor. "It takes time. The changes are not usually noticed until around six or seven months along," Dr. Begotka insisted.

Meanwhile, whenever I doubted, God continued to say to me in my daydreams, "Be patient, have faith." Wanting to see all our money and hard work pay off, I needed confirmation. As Beckett's first trimester report card showed little improvement, I hoped that was really God telling me to keep the faith and not my hopeful wishes. As I thought about that on my drive from work back to home, a radio commercial aired, saying, "Does your child have trouble in school? Perhaps your child has trouble reading, writing, and focusing on their schoolwork. If so, it may not be a learning disability or ADHD, which is often misdiagnosed. Perhaps your child has a functional eye issue. For a free screening, please call …" In shock, I almost skidded off the road. Never before in my life did I hear a radio advertisement for a functional eye problem. I literally laughed out loud as I looked up to God and thanked him for the obvious sign that gave me the confirmation that I needed.

A few months later, right around the six- or seventh-month mark of therapy, Beckett's teacher reached out, saying, "Beckett's hard work is paying off. He's just gone up three reading levels and is now proficient on the standardized tests. His focus in school is improving too. It's amazing. Keep up the good work."

And that was the start of our seeing the eye therapy come together. As I write this, Beckett's functional vision as well as his confidence in school continues to improve. For us, finding and treating it, was like finding a key to a treasure chest. With his eye function corrected, I'm beyond grateful that Beckett has unlimited treasure for the rest of his life.

Chapter 28: Purposeful Encounters

No one ever just walks into your life by accident. No one is just randomly there. They are there to play a role in the same way that you play a role in the lives of others. And sometimes, these roles aren't good – and you have to be okay with that.

— Anonymous

On a chilly, dark Saturday morning over Valentine's Day weekend, while my sister-in-law graciously babysat my children, I decided to make the most of my time alone and ventured to a thrift store — a place where I never had time to browse without screaming kids in tow. As I looked for hidden gems, a chance encounter wound up being what caught my attention the most. Jill, my pastor's wife and my past mentor mom from MOPS (mom's group), greeted me with a warm smile. I hadn't seen her in quite awhile, but every time our paths crossed, she radiated love, and her presence made me want to stay and chat with her for hours. With great wit and spunk, her sense of humor captivated me, but at the same time, she listened with sincerity and really cared to know how I was doing.

As a mentor mom in MOPS six years prior, Jill had a dysfunctional group to deal with at church. Many of the ladies gossiped and formed a clique. Excluded often myself, I looked forward to hearing Jill share her wisdom and advice on motherhood, as well as her spiritual journey through life. I felt a strong soulful connection with her, but the setting didn't provide the fertile environment for a friendship to grow. Unfortunately, it felt like a middle or high school class because the women often talked over her as if they were more interested in themselves than the topic of the meeting. Furious, I refused to go back as well for the same reasons. After this group fell apart, Phil encouraged me to reach out to Jill to seek her advice on how to deal with the fake Christians I kept encountering.

"I'm just not comfortable with that. She's too busy," I insisted.

"I don't know. I think you two would hit it off as you're both down to earth and real."

"I think we would too, but I don't want to bother her. What would we talk about? I don't have the Biblical knowledge she has. It's too intimidating," I replied.

"I also think she'd be a good person to bounce ideas off of for your book. You need someone like her in your life."

"She'd probably think the book is odd."

That conversation with my husband occurred six years ago and continued to recur after Jill's and my paths crossed at church from time to time. As much as I wanted to reach out, I assumed that she'd have no interest in a friendship with me.

Six years later, when I was at the thrift store, Jill's normally happy persona and beaming glow looked faded. As we talked, she explained how one of the high schools she subbed in was very dark and needed Jesus. "The teachers have bad morale, and the leadership doesn't seem very good. The teachers are fearful of administration. I'd like to get Young Life started there to help these students in their challenging times, but I'm not sure how with all the opposition going on there."

This led to my explaining how I landed my dream job at Emerson High School, which was a much better commute.

"Oh my gosh. That's great," Jill beamed.

With enthusiasm in how God worked, I said, "God used my past pain to help me learn how to listen to Him."

With a few tears in her eyes, she smiled and said, "God is so great. I'm so happy to see how the Lord is working in your life." As we parted ways, I saw a look in her eye that showed hope.

When I shared with my husband that night that I was fortunate to talk with Jill that day, he again badgered me to call her and invite her to coffee. For some reason, I just couldn't do it yet.

Two months later, I received a text which said, "Hey, this is Jill. I was wondering if we could get a cup of coffee over the weekend?" A text from Jill — shocked would be an understatement. How did she get my cell phone number? Why would she be texting me? Funny that she texted me after Phil had been saying for six years that I should reach out to her.

Chapter 29: Our First Coffee Meeting

The people who walk into your life are always going to be people who will be able to expose you to new perspectives; these are people who will offer you vast opportunity for growth and personal expansion. And it's up to you to take advantage of these opportunities.

— Anonymous

　　As I drove to our local coffee hang-out to meet Jill for the first time on an early Saturday morning, my stomach growled out of fear, and I wondered if I shouldn't cancel and turn around. I just could not imagine what we'd talk about, and why she'd be reaching out to me. But the minute she saw me, she smiled warmly, and we made small talk about the simplest things — what we had for breakfast, education issues, qualms with our husbands, etc... She, too, liked organic food, was careful about not having too much sugar in her diet, and preferred natural health solutions over Western medicine. We both didn't care for coffee, which was ironic since that was supposedly the purpose of our meeting. I shared some issues in teaching and education, which she could relate to as she once taught special education and currently subbed. And we connected over having husbands who often never tell us what went on from one moment to the next. To say the least, our conversation was comfortable, which put my mind at ease. We were like two long lost friends connecting again after many years of being apart.

　　When our conversation reached a natural six-second lull, she excitedly pulled out a green notebook that had post-it notes, arrows, and maps of all sorts of God projects she was working on. I wondered what I had to do with this matrix of drawings and scribbled notes.

　　"I want to help one of my students who is struggling to get a good score on his ACT test. Do you know anyone?" Jill asked.

　　"Actually, I do. I'll text you a name of one of my teacher friends who has a side business helping kids increase their ACT scores."

　　"Oh my gosh. That would be great. I've also been wanting to get a Young Life group started in this area. Do you have any thoughts on that or any connections where you teach?"

"Funny you should ask. I know some students who are looking to start a Bible group. They told me that because I read a chapter of my book on how God speaks, and they were all super interested."

"You're writing a book. Oh, look at this." This is when Jill dug through her purse and handed me the business card to a local writing group.

"This is crazy. How did you know?"

"Must be a God thing," Jill said as she smiled.

We went back and forth like that with connection after connection until we finally had to say goodbye. To think I questioned why we should get together. After this meeting, it was obvious to both of us that God brought us together to help encourage and inspire one another in our current journeys.

The next day at school, the Emerson Moms in Prayer group left a bunch of treats in the teacher's lounge for Teacher Appreciation Week. As I saw their special note to all of us, it said,

We want to encourage you in your great work of shaping the lives of our children, offering you this special treat and letting you know that you are prayed for regularly. We appreciate all you do! If there is any way that we can be of help to you, or if you have a specific prayer request, please let us know; either write it on the inside of this card or email it; prayer requests will be received and handled with complete confidentiality.

The minute I saw this, God whispered to me to take a picture of that note and send to Jill. I sensed that this prayer group would be a great way for her to seek advice in how to possibly bring Young Life to Emerson High School. Not long after passing on the information, Jill did contact them and received some helpful pointers. Finding this prayer group at just this time provided a needed sign that God was at work and that we both should keep going with what God wanted us to do.

After a few meetings with Jill, God told me that I should give a copy of my book to her to read. In my mind, I answered back, "Um, you do realize she is the pastor's wife and that she has a master's degree in Biblical studies herself? That's a bit intimidating. She may look at it and think I'm so off base."

And I heard right back in my mind, "That's exactly why you need to give her a copy and seek her advice." I knew God was right. Of course, He was. He is God and knows so much more, but I couldn't help wanting to resist doing what He asked. Sometimes it's easier to ignore God's promptings.

Weeks later, Jill texted me from one of her trips, saying, "Your book is great. So glad you are listening to God and doing this work. A book like this doesn't exist and is needed. Too many people go around thinking they have a relationship with God but really do not. Your book is a good reminder and example of how God speaks and wants a relationship with everyone."

That confirmation from someone whom I trusted and whom I perceived knew God's words better than I did fueled my confidence and stamina to keep writing.

Chapter 30: The Struggle for Truth

Forget what hurt you, but never forget what it taught you.
— *Shannon L. Alder*

The friendship that blossomed between Jill and me was clearly a Godsend — one of those rare gifts where someone just completely gets you, accepts you, and loves you unconditionally for reasons that even you yourself don't understand. What started as monthly coffee meetings to discuss our journeys through life, quickly turned into weekly meetings and daily phone or text conversations. Einstein, Emerson, and Thoreau would have been proud of our philosophical insights. Rarely light, we discussed highly debatable topics — theories of time and the idea that time does not exist, synchronicity, false prophets, Biblical truths, fake Christians, forgiveness, education, marriage, parenting, politics, mental illness, drug addiction, and our God callings, to name a few. She read the draft of this book, so discussing ideas of how God spoke to us became a central focus. God talked to both of us often, including through each other at random wake-up calls at three in the morning. Basically, anything that affected our lives or the lives of those around us became game for our daily texts. I trusted her with all my heart and soul, and as a result, felt I could tell her anything. She's what I'd call a "soul friend" sent from God. We'd encourage each other with music, Bible verses, philosophical ideas, truth-telling, and so on. According to Jill, we were "ninja friends," which meant we would help each other fight our daily battles through prayer, especially when Satan attacked and attack he did.

Over the months that our friendship budded, I secretly hoped she'd never find out just how inadequate I felt my Biblical knowledge was. In my mind, I believed that once she knew I didn't know the Bible like most of the Christian leaders at our church, she'd surely drop me. When I'd share those ideas with her, she quickly built me up saying that so many Christians go through the motions and may have the Biblical knowledge but become overly proud and don't live a life of listening to and obeying God.

"If you know one Bible verse well and live it, that will

be more than what most people do."

So there was hope for me yet. She taught me to pray my heart out loud, as well as to do a faith walk by breathing in positive affirmations and by breathing out negative ones. Sharing those spiritual ideas out loud proved difficult for me and made me uncomfortable at times, but she'd just encourage and laugh with me along the way, never judging or looking down on me.

At critical times, we lifted each other up — she was there, offering love and support when my extended family created silly drama; in her life, I came to her side when her son unexpectedly died. We shed lots of tears together and through it, reminded each other that God was the only one who understood and could take our pain away. A few nights after her son died, and I wanted some comforting, but not clichéd words to share with her and her family, God woke me up and asked me to write and share this with them:

Tell them to lean on me.
  I can take their pain and heartache.
  I will wipe their cleansing and healing tears.

Tell them I will be with them now, tomorrow
  And in the future. I am. Like the famous
  "Footprints" poem, I am carrying each of you,
  continue to lean on me.

Tell them I love them. And while each minute, hour, and day
  drags on filled with mist and fog,
  The sun will shine again, and joy will return to
  your hearts in time.

Tell them to forgive themselves. None of this is any
  of your fault. Let go of the things you could have
  said or done.

Tell them Eddie is with me in heaven at peace,
  sorry for things he has said or didn't do, but
  finally free from the clutches and madness of mental illness.

Tell them that while Eddie is physically gone
  he is still here, just as I am — for nothing ever dies.

Rejoice in the memories — the good times
and know that Eddie loves each of you.

While Jill let me and a few others help her in some of
the darkest moments of her life, four weeks after her son's
death, and immediately after his funeral, Jill's visits, texts, and
phone calls slowed down and then one day, just stopped.
Nothing. No sign. No warning. Just gone. It felt as if she died
from my life. I found myself grieving deeply. After all, she
was one of those rare gems in my life whom I loved and
trusted.

As the days lingered on and Jill continued not to text,
call, or ask to get together, my feelings of loss and hurt made
me question if we were ever truly friends at all. Had I been
deceived? Had she decided that I wasn't someone she could
associate with because I wasn't as far on the spiritual path as
she was?

After three weeks of feeling as if a close friend died, I
sat in church when a class called "Who Switched Off My
Brain?" was advertised in the announcements before service
started. It was to be held in five minutes in the church
basement. While waiting for service to start, God whispered,
"You need to leave church and go to this class now. You
won't regret it." I told Phil we had to go. He looked at me,
confused and a little bit in awe, saying, "Go ahead then."

"No, you need to go too. It's for both of us." Like a
magnet pulling me away, I left to attend this class, not having
the faintest idea of why I needed to go. The goal of the class
was to teach people to detox their brains and rid themselves of
harmful thoughts, emotions, and the stress they generate.
Perfect, right? Yep. I needed this class. It was so obvious. So,
in one session, I learned that I needed to capture my thoughts
because thoughts create our moods and attitudes. To capture
the thought, according to our instructor, Tracy, I had to focus
on the feelings I had. She explained how feelings will always
come before thoughts.

Tracy challenged all of us to think of something from
the past week that made us feel something. Immediately, I
thought of my paradoxical feelings toward Jill: the hurt, loss,
and anger I felt. Just thinking about it twisted my stomach and

hurt my brain. Then, Tracy made us go deeper. Figuring out my feelings was a piece of cake. What next, I thought a bit skeptically. She explained that the thoughts about the other person usually have some deep-rooted storyline about ourselves. And there it was, out in the open like a map of clarity … my feelings of inadequacy, my feelings that I was not good enough to be her friend in the first place. But where did that come from? Tracy told us to ask Jesus to reveal it as He will always want healing. So I asked. And then, like a dam holding back water, the floodgates opened. I couldn't stop crying. When did I lose my confidence and feel so betrayed, angry, hurt, and inadequate? So unloved and not valuable? Like layers being peeled away one by one, the memory surfaced and the images of miscarriage after miscarriage pierced my mind, letting my heart bleed in pain. My heart ached and felt tortured again. As the images presented themselves to me, Tracy took me out to the hall to discuss.

"Why are you crying? What are you feeling?" Babbling in tears, I explained how for ten years, I worked hard to have a biological child, and as each loss came, I felt God betrayed me, which made me feel deeply unloved as a result. While I wouldn't change anything now because I have the two biggest blessings through adoption, the memory created scars and mistruth that I believed and never let go of from that time. Not believing I was good enough was a lie that affected every aspect of my life. As I spoke with Tracy in the hall about my feelings of loss with Jill and where those thoughts stemmed from, she said, "The real truth is that you have value, you are lovable, and what's going on with Jill is not about you. She is just busy and can't be a friend to anyone right now."

As I went back into the room with the truth in my heart, God continued to heal me by whispering more truths. A few months back, God revealed to me through a dream that I sometimes have trouble forgiving others because I have not forgiven myself. I knew that was true but didn't know how to get to the core of why I couldn't forgive myself. I knew it had to do with my anger toward myself in all my miscarriages and falsely believed I had control over. I blamed myself. But knowing this intellectually was not enough. My heart didn't believe I should forgive myself.

On this random day, however, God finally made the truth crystal clear by connecting all the dots as he said, "Don't you see …

you're saying you are not good enough is getting in the way of your forgiving yourself. Now that you know the truth that you are good enough and deeply loved, you can forgive yourself finally." By changing my thoughts and saying, "I am good enough. I am loved," I could be free and heal. Being free meant I knew the truth, and by knowing that, I could look at other situations in a more accurate light like in my friendship with Jill.

A day later after this realization, a tight spot at the top of my neck that felt like rocks, finally loosened up and disappeared. Before this awakening of truth, for relief, I tried acupuncture, chiropractic, dry needling, yoga, and massage therapy without any luck. One day, my massage therapist said while working on my neck, "I really think your pain that is stuck in that spot is some type of emotional pain that you need to deal with. It's just not acting like normal muscle tightness. Perhaps you are holding onto something that you need to let go of." It appeared that my emotional thorn of lies affected my neck, and once that thorn released, healing began not only mentally, but physically. Five days after the realization I had at the brain class, I went back to my massage therapist, and while massaging me, she exclaimed with excitement, "What did you do to your neck? It's never been this loose, and it no longer feels like rocks. Amazing." I explained how I had some emotional pain like she suspected that I finally let go of and forgave myself for. We both were in awe at how that emotional pain affected my neck until I unlocked the secret lies I told myself.

Two days later while at a concert hearing Unspoken, Danny Gokey, and the Casting Crowns, God spoke to me while listening to "Just Be Held." The song reminded me of how no one is ever alone if we have a relationship with God. It felt like He said, "Here I am, and we have some things to talk about." God said in my heart, "You did nothing wrong. You think because she leaned on you before and now needs her space that this is a reflection of you, but it's not. Before, she was in shock and was busy taking care of her husband and everyone else. When she stopped responding to you, it was the first time she started to deal with her son's loss and all his affairs. Keep praying for her and lean on me when you feel lonely. Trust that she just needs time."

When I saw Jill at church two days later, she purposefully looked my way and waved to me from across the room. And so, like the years when I dated and even when I broke up with Phil for two weeks while we were engaged, I reminded myself that my friendship with Jill was like that famous cliché if you love something, let it go. If it does not come back, it was never meant to be." The scary truth about that statement was the idea that maybe this friendship was not meant to be, a truth I did not want to entertain. While I now have confidence that "I am good enough and lovable," I needed to cast the fear of loss out the door and close it forever. I realized that instead of fearing loss, I had to ground my thinking in faith, hope, and love, all while trusting God.

A few days later, I decided to see Tracy, the therapist who taught the brain class at church. She tried a technique called "EMDR" on me. According to the EMDR Institute, "EMDR (Eye Movement Desensitization and Reprocessing) is a psychotherapy that enables people to heal from the symptoms and emotional distress that are the result of disturbing life experiences. Repeated studies show that by using EMDR therapy, people can experience the benefits of psychotherapy that once took years to make a difference. EMDR therapy shows that the mind can in fact heal from psychological trauma, much as the body recovers from physical trauma. The brain's information processing system naturally moves toward mental health. If the system is blocked or imbalanced by the impact of a disturbing event, the emotional wound festers and can cause intense suffering. Once the block is removed, healing resumes. Using the detailed protocols and procedures learned in EMDR therapy training sessions, clinicians help clients activate their natural healing processes."

Waving her fingers back and forth in front of my eyes as I followed like a little lost puppy, she asked me to picture myself sad and upset as I looked at my cell phone and saw no texts back from Jill.

"How do you feel as you see this image?" Tracy questioned.

"I feel hurt, confused, and can't help wondering what I did wrong. On a scale of one to ten, I feel a ten in the sadness department."

"Keep thinking about that." Her fingers continued to go back and forth. "What else do you see and feel?"

"Not sure."

"Keep picturing Jill." Her fingers continued to go back and forth.

"I see Jill's sadness. Her brain is foggy. She can't think straight. Has no energy to do anything."

"How does that make you feel?" Tracy asked.

"Broken-hearted for her. I see all the good times we had. Her sparkly eyes of truth looking at me. But she's lost right now."

"What else?"

"I see other things too. Friends of the past who left. Dan who died on his motorcycle when we were twenty-three years old. I loved him and might have married him. Amelia who has been friends with me for decades and who hasn't been around the past few years due to a serious illness. She also needs to forgive herself for her abortion so she can heal. Fake friends who betrayed me for reasons I don't understand."

"Go on…"

"With Jill, I question whether she is a true friend."

"Stay with that thought." Her fingers continued to go back and forth as my eyes followed again. "Now what do you feel or see?"

"How do I know this is from God?" I interrupted.

"Just trust that it is. Say what pops into your head as God can talk like that."

"God is telling me that I can trust my judgment. Jill not texting me back is not about me. She needs to grieve privately and rely on God. It's not my fault."

"Go on with that thought that it's not your fault." Her fingers continued back and forth. "What do you feel?"

"I see the loss of Dan. I see all my miscarriages. I see Amelia."

"Let's ask Jesus to come in," Tracy said. "What does Jesus say?"

"None of these losses are your fault." The gate that held back my tears let loose as I cried uncontrollably for all my past losses. It felt like time from the past came and met me in the present. No time existed except for that moment. All my past miscarriages stared me in the face, telling me to forgive myself and let go. Nothing I could have done would have made those pregnancies work out. Something powerfully spiritual and beyond this world miraculously healed me through my cleansing tears. Each baby's face presented itself in my mind and said he or she was with God in Heaven. I'd see them again someday.

"What do you rate your sadness now?"

"A zero. I know none of this is about me. I don't have to take these things personally." As I said that, true joy and relief radiated in my heart. It was hard to believe that I went from a ten to a zero that quickly; it truly felt like pieces of lead had been removed from both my heart and brain, making me feel much lighter.

"God used your feelings of loss with Jill to heighten and stir up all your past feelings of hurt, betrayal, and past loss," Tracy explained.

I had to confront these losses from the past like a cavity without Novocain. God exposed Satan's huge lies — that I thought I did something wrong and that I thought I was not good enough. The trauma around my past finally released, and God used the situation with Jill to activate my past hurt. Knowing the truth set me free and healed the trauma that was stuck in my brain for years. For the first time, I didn't just intellectually forgive myself, but truly did so in my heart, which I could now do because I knew the truth that none of those losses were any of my fault.

"I fully believe that God used this situation to heal you and wanted Jill to stay away, so you'd have to confront all these past losses. God may be teaching her something too," Tracy said.

With a genuine smile on my face, I left, knowing that the friendship ending was not my issue and that it served a purpose for both of us in that season of life.

Before telling Phil what happened, he saw me an hour later and said, "You look different. Like you are happier and have white light all around you. What did Tracy do to you?"

"Well, I can tell you what God did …"

Two days later, while waiting for the movie *The Shack* to start, I retold this healing experience to a friend. "I just hope that Tracy is correct in that I'm healed."

"Did you ever think that God wanted Jill to go to Him for healing? And, while you both helped each other out, God wanted you to rely on Him to heal as well? Maybe this had to happen," Emily said.

"Wow, you're probably right. I just want a sign that things

will be okay."

"Um, Christine. Look at who is here. It's Tracy, your therapist. Wow. There's your confirmation."

Knowing how coincidences just don't exist, I wondered what God wanted me to know by having the therapist who just helped me unlock my deep-rooted pain sit in front of me at this movie. I read this book ten years prior and knew going into the movie that I loved the spiritual lessons in it but couldn't remember all the details of it. As I watched the main character, Mack Phillips, deal with the abduction and loss of his child, I couldn't help but connect to his sadness and how I lost so many babies before they were even born. In this movie, Mack learned to forgive himself through the visitation of three people who symbolized God, Jesus, and the Holy Spirit. When God clearly spoke to this man, saying, "This is not your fault," that's when the force hit me.

As I heard those words again, I let out some loud ugly cries that had people looking at and worried about me. I felt transported to another time and place. Just two days prior, I was in Tracy's office undergoing EMDR with those same words as I relived my hurt and pain with my ten years of miscarriages, with the loss of my friend Dan, and with other friendship betrayals. For years, I believed God did not love me since He didn't bless me with a biological child, and for over a decade, I falsely believed it was all my fault — that I just didn't trust God enough, and therefore, was punished with miscarriage after miscarriage. But like Mack in the movie, God healed me and revealed the truth.

After the movie, Tracy turned around and hugged me tightly, asking if I was okay.

"This is getting weird, but it's all God, right?"

"Yes. This movie is so much of your story. I just wanted to turn around and hug you when you were crying. God meant for us to be here tonight. See you tomorrow at the brain class."

That night, at 4 a.m., God woke me up to discuss all that happened.

"Do you realize that Tracy came into the theater right after you told Emily that you wanted a sign that things would be okay?"

"Oh yeah. That's right."

"Emily was right. That was confirmation for you. I want you to trust me and just let Jill be right now."

"Okay."

We talked like two old friends over coffee. "How did you connect to the movie?" God asked me.

"That none of my past was my fault. I can forgive myself now."

"Yes, but also that you are deeply loved and that I wanted to heal you. I want a relationship and want healing for everyone."

"Thank you for healing me."

"Please go write these details down."

"I will later. I'm tired."

"No, go now. You'll forget some of this. All this ties it together. You are healed and need to share this with others, so they can be healed through your story. You need to tell people that having a relationship with me is important, so I can help them too."

Stumbling in the dark, I made my way to the office where I wrote down this conversation.

The next morning in Tracy's brain class, she asked me to share my story of healing with the class. As I did so, I explained all the ways that God spoke to me and how I felt nothing but joy because I knew what I said was God's work and truth; I hoped that someone else might feel inspired by how God worked in my life. Someone who saw me at the start of the class said that she could tell something happened to me these past few weeks. I no longer carried darkness but had a spirit full of joy and gratitude. Again, confirmation that healing really happened.

Tracy told the class she couldn't believe how quickly God worked in my life and healed me. Curious myself, I later asked God why. He responded, "This is the closure you need to finish the book, which needs to be written and published soon to help lots of people. There are people who will read it who need to know that I want to heal them. I want a relationship with them. I want them to know they are loved. I'm going to use you through your writing to reach them. Are you okay with that?"

"Um, yeah. I don't really have a choice, do I?" I asked jokingly.

"You have a choice, but in your heart, you know this is what you must do. Everyone has his or her own purpose in life. This is yours."

As Jill's son died, my friendship with Jill temporarily died — an unexpected loss that I had to grieve. For whatever reason, my friendship provided a good distraction from her son's mental illness before he died.

Looking back, I see how I assumed that because of her role as a pastor's wife, I falsely held her to a high standard of someone who could never hurt me. That night, God whispered to me in one of my dreams, "You can't judge Christians by their titles. Everyone will disappoint you, but I won't. Rely on me." I believe in my heart that Jill never intentionally hurt me. Deepak Chopra, a famous spiritual philosopher, said, "In the process of letting go, you will lose many things from the past, but you will find yourself." God ended up using that loss of friendship for my good, helping me heal past trauma and false beliefs that were not from God.

PART VIII: Finding Grace and Learning Forgiveness

Because we are human, it is inevitable that we will let people down, or others will not meet our expectations. I've been guilty of expecting too much from other people, and then being upset with them when they didn't act how I wanted them to. It's a little unfair, actually, which is how I finally learned what grace truly means. Giving and receiving grace is still a journey for me. I don't have it all figured out yet, but hopefully, you'll give grace to me on that. Learning to forgive is one of the toughest lessons to master, but I've learned that forgiving ourselves and others is key for true healing and happiness.

Chapter 31: Prophecy-God Speaks Through Prophets

If any of you lacks wisdom, let him ask God, who gives generously to all without reproach, and it will be given to him.
— James 1:5.

I'm no expert on prophets or the idea of prophecy. As I've explained in my chapters on infertility and miscarriage, I've been burned by false prophets before (by both Beth and Mike) who basically said I'd have my own biological children once I trusted God and fixed things from my prior lives — past lives — whatever that meant. But the Bible showed that prophets existed and that the Holy Spirit talked through them, so the idea was worth entertaining. In the Bible, 2 Peter 1:19 says, "And we have the word of the prophets made more certain, and you will do well to pay attention to it, as to a light shining in a dark place, until the day dawns and the morning star rises in your hearts." I had to keep that idea in mind when my ladies Bible study group asked me to hear Zore speak, a well-known prophet who visited Wisconsin from Macedonia.

With hesitation, I piled into my friend's car and a group of us went to a house on Okauchee Lake where a man named Tim hosted Zore. At first, Zore did not say anything revolutionary — just a lot of Christian facts that made sense to me. He explained how "some things the Holy Spirit says are just for you; they can't be interpreted by others." Quoting 1 Corinthians 14:3, he explained how we needed to be strong in our faith with God before we could help others. To know God, we needed to know the Holy Spirit first, as the Holy Spirit lives inside each of us. While pastors and books can teach and guide us about God, we needed to have a relationship with the Holy Spirit ourselves. Once we knew the Holy Spirit, we could then start to get to know Jesus and God.

Zore went on to say, "You need to listen and speak to the Holy Spirit inside of you, and when you pray, ask in the name of Jesus. If the prayer is God's will, it will be answered." But sometimes, people feel ignored when we pray because prayers weren't always answered. If the prayer was not what the Holy Spirit wanted, it will not be answered. As Zore explained this, my mind flashed back to a conversation not too long ago with my Bible study ladies. One lady naively stated that "God is good and answers all prayers."

"That's not true. He didn't answer my prayer for biological children. I prayed for ten years, and that prayer was never answered."

"Oh, sure he did. You have two beautiful kids."

"I love my kids and would love them the same if they were my offspring, but they are not biological. That specific prayer was never answered."

"It's the same thing," my Bible study friend replied in a flippant manner.

"But it's not. God's will for me did not include my having biological children, and that's okay. I accept that now, but to say that God answers all people's prayers is not accurate. Finding my children through the gift of adoption was God's plan and answer to our prayer for us to have a beautiful family. God does not always answer our prayers how we want Him to, but in the end, God's answer through my two adopted sons was better than I could have ever imagined, so much so that I'm now thankful my original prayer was never answered."

As Zore continued to discuss God's will, I came back to reality, aware that it really was okay that God's plan for us didn't include biological children. Who knows ... maybe I would have died in childbirth, or maybe we would have given birth to a child with some severe issues that one or both of us would have trouble handling, or maybe the two children we have were meant to be our sons and brothers to each other. The possibilities for why things turned out as they did were endless, and the truth was that I would not ever know all those reasons but needed to trust that it was all in my best interest. There are reasons for everything, yet we won't always know them. Ironically, but not coincidentally, when I drove home that night, Garth Brook's famous song, "Unanswered Prayers" played, which made me smile and know that my not having biological children was truly okay and purposeful.

After Zore discussed how the Holy Spirit talked to people, he asked if he could go around the room and give a prophecy to those the Holy Spirit led him to. As the Holy Spirit advised him on what to say to various people, I knew that what he told many of my friends was true and unique to them. Zore finally came to me. Skeptical, I listened ... Zore said, "Ahhh, Christine. You are a runner. Not necessarily the sport of running (that's good because while I run, I hate it)." He quoted Paul from the Bible, saying, "I run for the reward. You are a trophy hunter. You have high goals and are a driver. You drive things and make them happen. For you, purpose is very important. If you go to something, you want to know the cause, reason, purpose, goal, etc ...You don't like to waste time. You'd be a great director of a company. But you are also a gentle, precious person. I see your hands. Not the physical hands, but what's underneath. You have hard working hands and are not afraid to accomplish things. You'll get the job done. But get to know grace and ask God to reveal it to you. When you don't live in grace, you try, and every time you try or strive, things get hard. You need to go with the flow and think of the simple things. You have a very developed brain and imagination. Ask the Holy Spirit to help you focus on the simple things, so you can relax and not worry. I have a Bible verse for you that the Holy Spirit wants you to focus on — Philippians 4:6. 'Do not be anxious about anything, but in every situation, by prayer and petition, with thanksgiving, present your requests to God.'"

After Zore said this to me and went on to reveal other people's prophecies, I sat, dumbfounded by what I just heard. What did this mean? He was right about my persistent personality and that I'm someone who works very hard for whatever goal I set. I didn't think he'd get that from just looking at me. And the Bible verse he quoted was ironically the same one that I was given by one of my friends at some point in my infertility and adoption journey. Several times, I found myself anxious and upset as I had to learn to accept things as they were and give thanks, even when my world looked downright depressing. Learning to have gratitude in the worst of times helped me see glimmers of joy in the midst of my constant tears. What really struck me, though, was the part about grace. What did that mean? While everyone else completely understood and embraced their messages given to them, I felt confused and even agitated that I'd let a prophet say anything to me again, especially after my prior experiences with them.

After the meeting, I insistently said to Zore, "What do you mean by my needing to get to know grace? Didn't God say anything about my writing a book? That's where I feel I really need help and guidance."

"I don't know what the Holy Spirit means. I can't know everything, and you can't either. Maybe in time, you will know what this means. I saw your hands hard at work. Maybe that's the book. Maybe it's for the future. But I do know that you can't worry about trying to have everyone understand your book. Those who are meant to understand and read it will."

Ticked off, I went home and found this verse in the Bible: "Above all, you must understand that no prophecy of Scripture came about by the prophet's own interpretation. For prophecy never had its origin in the will of man, but men spoke from God as they were carried along by the Holy Spirit" (2 Peter 1:20-21). So that explained how Zore couldn't know everything he told me. It's for me to figure out, which I hesitantly accepted as truth. In the past, Mike's and Beth's egos would get in the way, and they had an answer for everything. For the message to be real, though, it needed to come from the Holy Spirit. I had to test it. Through my relationship with the Holy Spirit, I asked for the meaning to be made clear.

To me, grace meant that I believed Jesus died for my sins and that I was forgiven. That I could go to heaven because I believed in him; to give grace to other people and forgive them for we all mess up all the time. But grace, in this context and the way I understood grace, didn't seem to make sense with what Zore said.

Weeks later, while writing and meditating about the topic, clarity hit me over the head. Because I work hard and strive to reach high goals, I'm often my own worst critic. My perfectionism gets in the way of my joy and living in the present moment. I needed to give myself grace like God gave me. I needed to be okay with letting go and not being perfect, and not trying so hard that I'm afraid to fail. Failing and learning from failure is what makes people grow and blossom into who we are meant to be. Figuring this out was not something anyone else could have explained. It was not directly in the Bible or any other book, but rather, I had to live it and pray about it to figure out. That's just what God wanted me to do. In the end, what Zore said to me appeared to be right on, but the difference between him and others who claimed to know truth was that I had to figure out by myself how the Holy Spirit's words applied to my life.

Chapter 32: God's Answers Come in His Perfect Timing

God is never late and rarely early. He is always exactly right on time — His time.

— Dillon Burroughs

On an ordinary Thursday night in June while at my husband's softball game, my dad called, letting me know that he checked into the hospital with complaints of shortness of breath, chest and arm pain, and an irregular heartbeat — hmmmm — all classic symptoms of a heart attack. As is typical with some men, my dad is one of those strong-willed guys who hadn't been to a doctor in over twenty years, so the fact that he even went to the doctor told me that something wasn't right. He didn't want to stay overnight at the hospital, and he insisted that he still planned on going to the graduation party for our relatives on Saturday, only two days later. As he fought with my mom and his doctors that he was going to go home any minute, he continued to say that he just had indigestion from some pie that he ate at work. The blood tests did not show any heart attack markers, which seemed strange to me, considering his symptoms. Meanwhile, as my mom explained my dad's stubbornness to me, God kept telling me to insist to my mom that he stay at the hospital as blockages would later be found. That night in my dreams, God said, "It's going to be scary, but I'm with you all. Be still and know that I am." I kept hearing that all night, not quite understanding. Then, a 5 a.m. wake-up call from my mom shed some light.

"They tried to do an angioplasty, and it failed. Dad has too many blockages, so they are going to transfer him to Waukesha Memorial Hospital where he will have a quadruple bypass."

"Whaaaaattt?" I asked, confused.

"Yes, the heart attack didn't show up at first in the blood work, but did later, as is often the case, I guess," my mom calmly explained. I couldn't understand how she could be so calm, but in hindsight, I believe we were both so in shock and in survival mode to figure out our next steps.

I darted out of bed, dressed, and dropped the boys off at daycare. The hospital was thirty minutes away, but it took

Phil and me just a little over twenty minutes. Upon arrival, the kindest ER receptionist showed me to the ICU waiting room. No record of Dad. Immediately full of panic, I called Mom and found out they were still at the Oconomowoc Hospital, which was thirty minutes away. So, Phil and I jumped back in the car and frantically drove to Oconomowoc. I just had to see my dad and feared that he could die at any moment. When did I see him last? What was the last thing we said to each other? I told him I loved him. That was good, but I couldn't fathom losing him now. Not at this point in my life. The thirty-minute drive to Oconomowoc felt like days to get there.

Finally, we arrived. No record of him existed there either. Unbelievable. Where the heck was my dad? And if there was no record of him in a hospital operating room or some other room, what did that mean? As I asked the receptionist in our hometown hospital to keep looking, she found that he was never checked into a room and was just in the ER all night. Another nurse explained how he was just transferred back to Waukesha where we just came from. We again jumped back into the car and sped to Waukesha. If the police were to pull us over, I had my sob story planned out and would ask them to escort me to the hospital. Maybe we could get there even faster. I kept worrying about whether I would see my dad alive again. Fear continued to wrap its ugly hands around me. For whatever reason, my mom did not answer her cell phone either. Almost emotionally paralyzed, I couldn't help but think the worst.

At the time, I had a close group of friends whom I met with every two weeks for a Bible study. The group of us were together for about three years and did many social things over that time — from celebrating birthdays, to cheering on the Badgers or Packers, to going to Christian concerts and retreats. They were supposedly "my tribe" — people I could trust and count on in both the good and bad times of life. We also had a group app where there would be several (and when I say several, I mean there could be up to 50 texts or more) per day with ladies sharing funny stories of their kids, husbands, or life trials. Sometimes, the texts involved urgent prayer requests from the everyday stress of life or from crisis situations.

As I felt numb, alone, and scared in the car, driving back and forth, looking for my dad and knowing the situation was as serious as it could get, I asked these ladies to pray. I explained my frustration in not knowing what his condition was, but that I was determined to find out. One well-meaning lady wrote, "Christine, praying for him, but remember to be the light. Trust God. He's got this."

Be the light? Trust God? What I needed was an empathetic friend. While I knew being a Christian meant that people need to live a Godly way, and at times, be a role model of how Jesus would act, my goal was not to spread my Christianity at that moment. I desperately needed to find my dad, figure out what the heck happened, and make sure that the doctors were doing all they could for him. And while I knew God was in control, trusting him didn't mean that my dad would be okay or that he would live through his heart attack and possible complications. I sure learned that lesson from my infertility journey. The advice to "trust God" felt trite without the compassion I needed.

When I finally reached the ICU waiting room again in Waukesha, no record of my dad existed. I couldn't believe nor understand it. Not knowing if my dad were dead or alive consumed my every thought. Half an hour passed with no news. Nothing at all. My world stopped. Time again was relative and didn't exist, yet everyone else moved around like it was a normal day. It wasn't their dad fighting for his life. The volunteer who was supposed to figure out where Dad was in the ICU didn't appear to care as he read his paper and showed little empathy or emotion. Seeing people's families worried and at the end of their ropes was part of the volunteer's life every day. Crying and thinking that Dad was in some emergency surgery, I ran back to the welcoming and kind ER receptionist whom I met earlier, the same one who said her dad had a heart attack. She understood the panic I felt. Without any hesitation, she walked me to the ICU and showed me to his room. He had one? Why didn't anyone tell us?

And there he was. Dad helplessly lay in a hospital bed, scared, while going through tests to figure out all that was wrong with him — newfound diabetes, four blocked arteries, and who knew what else. The doctor asked a series of questions:

"Did you ever have any blood clots?"

"No," said Dad confidently.

Dad's "no" didn't sound right to me. A little voice in my head chimed in and said, "Tell them about the Factor V Leiden you found during your infertility and miscarriage work-up. You inherited that blood clotting disease from him."

Even though that seemed strange to me, I said, "I have Factor V Leiden, a blood clotting disorder that was found with my miscarriages. My mom was tested and does not have it, so that means I inherited it from my dad."

With concern all over his face, the hematologist said, "That's very important information and puts your dad at a 70 times greater chance of having a blood clotting related complication before, during, and after surgery. Now we can prepare for it with blood thinners and take the necessary precautions." Without the proper thinning of his blood, my dad had a good chance of a serious complication.

Ten years prior to my dad's heart attack, I found out I had Factor V Leiden. At that time, many well-meaning people said that I found the missing link to solving my infertility journey, and that with Lovenox (blood thinner) shots, I'd have a successful pregnancy. It worked for many others, so friends and relatives assumed it would be my solution. In the back of my mind, I kept thinking how that information was not for me. It was just a piece to a puzzle, but I still didn't have all the pieces or even know what the puzzle was to look like. I never understood why I figured out I had Factor V and what that meant for me. Of course, I wanted that to be my solution. It seemed to be an easy fix. After all, God led me to find out the information and also told me to remember it for later. One doctor even said, "Factor V is the number one reason for blood clots and heart attacks. Be sure to have your whole family tested."

Even years ago, the idea came across my mind that this information was not for me, but perhaps life-saving information for someone else one day, and now that day arrived. I hoped and prayed that knowing this information would be the key to saving Dad's life. Each day felt like a ticking time bomb. At any moment, my dad could have had a massive heart attack. He needed the emergency surgery to unclog the four blockages, but unfortunately, he couldn't have the surgery until his blood sugar came down closer to 100 and until his blood was thinned enough to prevent the blood clotting from the Factor V Leiden.

On pins and needles, I reached out again to the Bible study group for support. I received a few messages that people were praying for my family, but many didn't respond at all. After setting my pride aside and asking for help, which was difficult for me to do, no one in the group offered to watch my kids or help with meals like they did with other people in the group when they went through challenging times. Later, they said they thought someone else would do it. And one lady said, "Why don't you ask people at church for help?" Ask church for help? They were the church. I wasn't going to have strangers watch my kids. Unfortunately, the friends and family who wanted to help us lived out of state. Everyone's life went on as normal while mine felt permanently paused. Each minute felt like hours, hours felt like days, and days felt like weeks. I felt as if I were in another universe and time zone.

After a successful quadruple bypass, my dad again had complications with pain, A-fib (atrial fibrillation), diabetes, and blood clotting concerns. We were not out of the woods by any means and having a stroke was a common complication that the doctors were on guard for. Scared again that we could lose him, I texted my Bible study group, giving them the update and request for prayer. I asked them if anyone was free to do something that night as I had been at the hospital for over a week and needed to get out and get my mind off things. Most of them texted back, saying they would pray, but that they had plans for the night.

In need to get out of the house, I went to Saturday night church. It couldn't be a coincidence that Pastor Tom spoke about how we will all have seasons of pain and joy, but through everything, we need to trust in God. Trust again? I cried out of pain, out of knowing that he was right, and out of knowing that was all I could do. However, no amount of tears changed how helpless I felt. After the service, Pastor Tom came over and asked me what was wrong. Pastor Tom was right. Trusting in God did not mean things would go my way but that I had to trust that God would help us get through whatever we were being given in this stressful and trying situation.

When I came home that night, there were supportive texts from my best friend, Amy, whom I'd been friends with for over forty years, another one from my college friend Tori whom I'd known for twenty plus years, and a meal from an unexpected local mom friend who surprised me with her kindness. All these gestures of love and support came on the same night where I later saw pictures on social media of my entire Bible study group at a summer night party. I had not been invited, even after I asked if any of them were free that night. I later talked to the friend who did not invite me. Her response bothered me more than not being invited. She said, "I just invited my closest friends. I don't think we need to invite everyone every time we do something. And to be honest, you've been needy lately." Needy? Of course, I was. My dad was in the hospital, fighting minute by minute for his life. The fear of losing him threw me into a psychological mess. What I needed at that time were friends who wanted to be there for me with empathy and compassion.

I later read author Ritu Ghatourey, who said, "It's during the worst times of your life that you will get to see the true colors of the people who say they care for you." The honest truth was that I had my family, a handful of relatives across the country and only a few friends who were really there for me. As I reflected with gratitude on my blessings, I realized that it's not about the number of friends I have, though, as much as it is about the quality. I had wonderful people in my life, but during that crisis, I felt very alone as most of those who truly cared and loved me lived far away and could only be there in spirit. God reminded me to be grateful for the few real friends and family I had who did reach out, and how this situation showed me who they were, a truth that was difficult to swallow, but important to know.

In terms of the Bible study group, I took a step back and didn't initiate any social gatherings with them for awhile. More people continued to join the group, and it went from nine to fifteen ladies in a matter of weeks. Cliques formed, and the ones I was once closest to created their own "group" app. They let the one I was on only be used for business type conversations regarding what day/time the group would meet. From there on out, I was included in the Bible study meetings, but no longer the social gatherings. I no longer had a "tribe" as they say.

Disappointed, shocked, and hurt, I questioned God. I questioned the behavior of Christians. I questioned how I could ever trust anyone again. I didn't understand how my "tribe" could vanish so quickly, especially since they called themselves Christians.

As I thought about all my questions, I read in Jen Sincero's book, "What other people think about you has nothing to do with you and everything to do with them … do not waste your precious time giving one single crap about what anybody else thinks of you … get booted from the tribe and find another one." It seemed a message meant for me — God working through someone's words in a book again. Even though I felt hurt and betrayed by people I thought were my friends, I knew I couldn't ever go back to that Bible study. I learned a long time ago from the famous author Maya Angelou that "when people show you who they are, believe them." Ignorance truly was bliss, but I had knowledge, and with that knowledge, I needed to let go of this tribe.

Without a doubt, I was disappointed by the ladies in my beloved Bible study group whom I felt let me down and whom I helped in their time of need. The pattern went on for awhile. Why? As months passed, God showed me through things I read and through dreams I had that the pattern continued because my expectations were too high. That didn't mean I should stay with people who were not being true friends. But it meant perhaps that prophet Zore was onto something when he said I needed to learn grace. I didn't understand it until months later. As I prayed over and over, asking God what I was to learn through the pain of the Bible study group gone bad, he finally said to me, "People will always disappoint you. You need to turn and rely on me. When your dad had his heart attack, you had to trust me." As this same answer came to me while I prepared for the day, my husband woke up at 3 a.m. with a message from God. Now, nothing normally would wake him up. He's not one to go to the computer and write something. He hates writing. However, he dragged himself to the computer anyway. Look at what he wrote:

> *Lord, help me to forgive others when they don't live up to my expectations. I know that you have to do that with me all the time. I am human like them and fall short and do not live up to others' expectations as well. We all live in this fallen world, but thanks to you and your forgiveness of us, it gives us a roadmap on how to forgive others, no matter what. Forgiveness does the body good! Take any unforgiveness in my heart and melt it away, so I may live a life you would want for me. Amen.*

The day I received that message from God through Phil, it had been one and a half years since I spoke to Jill and eight months since I left the Bible study group. I forgave Jill and felt ready to move on, so I texted her, asking if we could meet for coffee. No response. I asked her husband in church that day if she received my text.

"You see ... she's an extreme introvert and needed time to process the grief of our son who died."

"But why didn't she let me know? Why did she stop talking to me for no reason? It doesn't make sense." I thought I let all my pain regarding Jill go, but apparently, another layer of grief existed.

Pastor Tom said warmly, "I don't know. But I do know she loves you and that you came to her at a time in need. Sometimes there are just seasons of friendships and gratefully, you were there at one of the worst times of our lives. We needed you. Thank you for being a good friend."

I left the church, crying, not knowing how to make sense of it all, but knowing in my heart this was bigger than me and not something I may ever understand.

Knowing that my goal was to forgive and let go, it didn't seem like a coincidence. God spoke through Phil to give me the prayer that I needed to help heal past hurts as well as a lesson in relying on Him. As humans, we will often let people down, and half the time won't ever know about it. Ironically, six months later, Jill texted, "Hi. wondering if we could meet for coffee sometime? It's been awhile." For months, our schedules did not align, but after hugging and talking to her at church briefly, I felt true forgiveness without understanding what happened. Years later, God crossed our paths again, and our friendship has been rekindled.

God didn't reveal the whole road map when I found that important health information during my infertility, which shows how God sometimes gives us pieces of information, and if we pay attention, we can piece the puzzle together at just the perfect time. My dad's life was saved with a successful bypass surgery, and I feel extremely fortunate that my Factor V Leiden information helped the doctors save my dad's life, especially with the complications that happened after surgery. I will be forever grateful. Not only was I thankful for God's roadmap in this situation, but I also learned how to forgive and show grace when other Christians let me down. Jen

Sincero summed it up perfectly in her book saying, "Release all expectations, let everyone off the hook, treat people as a blank slate over and over again; expect only the best from them regardless of what they've done in the past, and you may be surprised. What you focus on, you create more of, and if you keep expecting people to annoy you, they will not let you down."

Ch. 33: God Reminds Me Who I Am

It takes courage to grow up and become who you really are.
— *ee cummings*

Having taught for over two decades in several school districts, I encountered every type of leader you could imagine — the micromanager, the dictator, the laissez-faire hands-off delegator, the charismatic schmoozer, and the democratic coaching leader. When my favorite principal, Mitch, decided to retire after having led our school for many years, I wondered who would direct our mother ship. In truth, most of the veteran teachers became anxious, saying that no one could come close to walking in his shoes after putting our school on the map as one of the best in the nation. Mitch truly understood and knew how to motivate people as he modeled excellence in all that he did. He paid attention to the details, so that they never became big issues. He made each one of us feel that we mattered by making a point to acknowledge and compliment our contributions. Even when he needed to hand out constructive criticism, he did it in such a way that we all ended up agreeing with him and wanting to do better to please him. We all secretly felt we were his favorite — a true testament to his great leadership and people skills.

When the new sheriff, Brett, came to town, everything changed; I no longer felt valued at work. No longer were emails answered in a timely manner. No longer were our efforts noticed or praised, and no longer were employees given the benefit of the doubt when something came up with a student or parent concern. Like an expert gambler, Brett held his cards with a poker face. I never knew where I stood with him until one day, when he blindsided me and came into my classroom to talk.

"So, Christine. I want you to know that some students from one of your classes came down to complain," Brett said matter-of-factly.

"What about?"

"I can't really share that with you, or else I'll break their trust. But know that you should be aware that some don't like how you grade while others think you ask them to write about deep topics," he said.

Upset with the vagueness of his answer, I wanted clarity. "I don't understand. Can you give me specifics?" I practically begged.

"Well, just reflect on it, and I'm sure it will make sense to you," Brett suggested.

Make sense to me? What? I felt pretty sure it wouldn't ever just come to me. I replied, "If you want me to improve something, I'm happy to, but I need to better understand what you're talking about. I'm sure there are lots of students who think they wrote a piece better than they did. Not everyone is always going to be happy with the grade they receive, but if you send them to me, I can explain their grades, or help them to improve their writing."

"Well, aren't there lots of ways to grade something?"

"I'm not sure what you mean. There are standards and criteria on rubrics that I teach to, as does any English teacher."

"I see. Well, just reflect on all of this. I also think you can be more innovative in how and what you teach."

"What do you mean by that?" I asked, trying not to be defensive, especially since he had only been our principal for five months and never saw me teach.

"Um, I just want you to think out of the box. Do things that are outside of this classroom, and be authentic," he said.

As he left, I shook my head in disbelief. This new leader didn't know me and made disastrous assumptions based on hearsay, rather than based on my many years of successful student achievement and rapport that I had every year with most of my students. Why didn't he know I was one of the few who led the department in our new initiative with a reading and writing workshop at the high school level? And to question my level of innovation stung as I prided myself on being creative and designing authentic lessons and assessments. In fact, many other teachers came to me for new ideas and help with lessons. With my ego shot down and belittled, I didn't know what to think or do. I felt lost.

Over the next few months, Brett continued to see me through a negative lens, often stating what he thought were facts from a student or parent complaint without allowing me to share my side of a story. It appeared that he did not support most of his teachers, especially me, and as a result, thoughts of quitting my dream job crossed my mind each day. One night, as I lay in bed, frustrated with how I felt I couldn't win at work, I asked God for a sign to know whether I should stay or look elsewhere. And then right on my social media feed on my phone, I spotted a profound quote from Oprah that said, "Don't be confused between what people say you are and who you know you are." I smiled, knowing God intended for me to see that at just that time. In my heart, I knew I was an effective English teacher and a favorite to some. Years of experience and testimonials convinced me of that fact. But why must I come under such harsh criticism with a new boss? Why did I care so much what he thought of me when I knew the truth?

That weekend, I took my children to see the new Disney's *Lion King* movie. As I sat, watching and listening to "Hakuna Matata," God came in my daydreams and started chatting. "See, there are no troubles or worries."

"But there are," I whined back in my head.

Silence. The movie continued. Then Mufasa's ghost said to Simba, "You have forgotten who you are and so have forgotten me. Look inside yourself, Simba. You are more than what you have become."

Tears poured out and God spoke again inside my mind, "Remember who you are. You can overcome these challenges. Do not worry."

"But who am I?"

"Listen to your heart. You know."

Listen to my heart again? That's funny. Been there, done that. I laughed to myself thinking that was how I ended up in teaching in the first place! Since the school year only had a few weeks left until summer vacation, I knew I could suck it up and make it until the end. Maybe with the summer months and a fresh start to a new school year, things would get better. My heart, anyway, did not say I should quit — not yet anyway.

After a busy summer of chauffeuring my kids to and from each camp, sports or fun activity — I swear they lived their best lives — I welcomed the routine of school again. After just three weeks into the school year, Brett called me to his office. Not again, I thought.

"Christine, I want you to know that I realize at the end of a semester or year, you have great rapport and students like and respect you. We love the rigor and achievements your students have after having you. We can tell from the students' test scores that they learn so much from you. We don't want any of that to change. But there have been several students who have come down to complain that they are scared and that your class is too hard. Somehow, you need to be easier on them, yet keep your rigor and results that you get," Brett said.

"Can you explain what students are complaining about? I think it's normal that they complain at the beginning of a year before they know me because some of the students had middle school experiences where they were not held accountable. I hold them accountable for doing their homework and for good behavior. In a few weeks, they will adjust," I explained. And I also couldn't help but think that a few complaints should be a sign that I was doing something right.

"I want you to reflect on what you're doing and change it. Maybe give students surveys and see how they feel about you and your classes. Thank you."

Dumbfounded and beyond agitated with the lack of support and specific feedback to improve, I contemplated walking out and never coming back. In tears, I sought advice from Brett's supervisor, Jim. He knew me well as a person and as a teacher.

"What do I do? Anyone can go down and say anything at any time. I'm guilty by perception."

"It does appear that way. I think we need to have a meeting where we all put our cards on the table and confidentially talk about who said what. You can't improve unless you know the truth."

Exactly! A meeting with Brett, Jim, and myself was set for a week later. The day before the meeting, I met with Diana, my neck whisperer. Neck whisperer, you ask? Yep. On the anniversary of Dan's death on August 6th, I twisted my neck strangely while getting out of bed and jammed it so badly that I couldn't turn my head left or right for months. This was a new neck injury and on the other side of the neck than the injury I had years prior. Over time, I was able to move my neck better, but a knot the size of two quarters stayed put where my neck meets my skull. It always felt like a ball of tension, aching and stiff, and sometimes caused agonizing headaches. I tried chiropractic care. No luck. Massage. No luck. Dry needling. No luck. And now — physical therapy with the famous neck whisperer, Diana. Okay. She's not really called that, but that's my nickname for her.

Diana caught me off guard one session, saying, "Let's try some cranial sacral therapy. I'm thinking that maybe your neck has some emotional component. Maybe your body is holding onto physical pain due to some past emotional trauma. Is it okay if we do a little cranial sacral?"

"Sure. Go crazy," I said, hoping something might work. Diana had me lie on the table on my back as she put her hands under my skull. I didn't know what she was doing, but I felt my head get warm and felt energetic electric vibrations that felt like something moved around, loosening something up.

"What do you see or feel?" Diana asked.

"I don't know."

"Just say what comes to mind and trust it," Diana encouraged me.

"Well, I am getting a message. Know who you are," I said.

"What else?" she asked.

"Something about grace and forgiveness," I said.

"What does that have to do with?" Diana asked.

"Well, I have a meeting tomorrow at work that could be difficult. I feel unsafe at work and not trusted as an experienced teacher, and I'm often too hard on myself."

"I see you going into that meeting being confident, knowing you are meant to be a teacher."

With tears in my eyes, I knew God gave me a sign to be confident for my meeting. To sum up a long story, I went into the meeting with 170 student surveys, all with glowing reviews, I explained how I felt I was not being given specifics, did not feel safe or valued and that if things didn't change, I'd find another job.

Shockingly, Brett apologized and said, "Shame on me for judging you without ever seeing you teach. I will get in and observe you soon. Also, those students who complained about you now say that they like you, so in the future, I'll send students back to you or tell you about concerns as they happen."

That was a start. I didn't automatically trust Brett but hoped for the best and wanted to move forward. A few days later, I was back in Diana's office for my neck pain. It loosened up for a few days after the last session, but the pain quickly came back, haunting me again.

"Let's try this again and see if we can go deeper," Diana said. "What do you see and feel?"

"The phrase, 'speak your truth' comes to mind," I said.

"What's that about? I thought you just did that at your work meeting," Diana questioned.

"I did. But I see this is about the book I'm writing. Of course, that's what this is about. The neck pain came on the anniversary of Dan's death. This is all connected somehow," I said.

"What else is coming?"

"I'm worried about how my book will be received. So I write it and then put it away and stop. But God is saying it's the truth and needs to come out," I said.

"I'm getting a message. It doesn't matter if it's not well-received. Those who need it will love your book. The truth is not always well-received, but what you are writing is truth," Diana said. "I'm asking the pain if it can go away. It's saying it's here to remind you of your purpose."

I continued to feel warmth, and my neck loosened up more. I felt like I floated in the heavens as I saw bright yellow and white light. It was a lovely and peaceful image. Meanwhile, I heard Diana sniffling. "What's wrong?"

"I don't understand what I'm seeing. There's a vision of heaven. And light, and clouds and lots of babies. They are all around you. And it's like you are birthing something. Any idea what this means?"

I started crying too. "Um, I think it's all the past babies that I miscarried. They are all still with me?"

"I think so. There's energy from them. They are reminding you to write. You are basically birthing a book. Let's ask them to leave your neck alone."

My neck broke out in a sweat, and I felt like I was in a sauna with all the energy around me.

"They say they won't leave until your book is done. The pain is connected to your past trauma and when you birth the book, the energy will be released and your neck may feel better, hopefully," Diana said.

My mind couldn't believe what I heard. As I sat up and shared more of the story of what happened in my infertility journey,

Diana said, "I am positive that I saw lots of babies and the idea of birthing something." Just as she said that, a lullaby song came on over the sound system in the clinic that was connected to the hospital.

"What's that?" I asked, startled.

"Um, that would be the signal that a baby was just born." We both laughed.

"Unbelievable! And that's obviously a message for you too. Your book is like a baby in process too," Diana said excitedly.

And God whispered in my ear, "It will happen. Don't doubt this!" I smiled inside, knowing that without a doubt, God was with me, guiding me toward my soul's purpose.

When I went home that night, I graded some student papers, and my jaw dropped reading what one of my students wrote when quoting Paulo Coelho's novel *The Alchemist*, saying, "You will never be able to escape from your heart. So it's better to listen to what it has to say." It seemed that message to "listen to my heart" was one I never could escape and that again, I was given a sign to embrace this gift instead of trying to run away from it.

A few weeks later, Disney's *Frozen II* came to the theaters, and of course, with great anticipation, I wondered what new theme song would attract or annoy the world like "Let it Go" did in the first movie. As I sat in the theater, watching the movie with my kids and laughing at Olaf's funny jokes, especially the one about turtles breathing through their butts, I didn't expect to gain deep, spiritual wisdom. But as Anna said to Elsa, reminding her of her powers, saying, "When will you see yourself as I see you?" and then later telling her, "I believe in you, more than anyone or anything," I felt reminded of how God said the same to me numerous times. At one point in the movie, Pabbie reminded Elsa to "Be careful. The Spirits will challenge you every step of the Way." Later in the movie, when Elsa realized that "Fear is what can't be trusted," God said in my mind that I needed to let go of my fear with writing and publishing my book. I would be challenged in the process, but I needed to keep going. Fear, after all, is the opposite of trust. If I let fear rule me, I'm not really trusting God or his plan for my life. This reminder was reinforced later in the movie when General Mattias said to Anna, "Be prepared. Just when you think you found your way, life will throw you into a new path." Anna asked what to do when that happens, and General responded, "Don't give up. Take it one step at a time." I almost couldn't believe what I heard. As the characters reiterated the conversation I just had with God, my heart smiled at another confirmation that God wanted me to know and understand this. So with that confirmation, I went home and signed up with a writing coach that same day.

That following weekend, I attended a craft fair where I met Lisa, an author of a published Christian children's book. She encouraged me to join their Christian fiction writer's group and asked to see a sample of my writing. After sending her my first chapter, she wrote me, saying:

> *Nice message. I see you have lots of work to do and a long way to go. Who is your audience? You need to think about that. That's something a publisher will ask you. Honestly, I probably would never read something like this unless it were divided up into sections. You should hire an editor. Don't worry. We all use editors to make our writing better. I'm not sure if our group would help you or not but come if you like. Best of luck.*

Wow. That was super encouraging — not. I knew my draft needed some work, but for someone I didn't know to just come out with such negativity and little encouragement bothered me. Wasn't she interested in what God said to me? I went back and forth between believing I was a writer and feeling that I was some phony who didn't have a chance. Lisa reinforced my worst fear — people would not want to read this, so why waste my time?

I continued to work on my writing, but now with doubt. Who was I to think I was a writer? I didn't know it at the time, but I had "imposter syndrome," a common syndrome among creative people. Austin Kleon wrote in his book, "it means that you feel like a phony, like you're just winging it, that you really don't have any idea what you're doing." Yep, that was me and my writing for sure!

A few weeks later, my imposter syndrome was put to the test again, but this time at a Star Wars movie that my cousin in Chicago begged me to see with our kids over our Christmas break. I'm not a huge Star Wars fan. I hardly know the relationships between all the characters. To be honest, I went thinking I'd sleep through the movie. But early on in the movie, Leia said, "Rey, never be afraid of who you are."

God whispered to me, "Are you listening?"

"Um, yes. Now you're talking to me through a Star Wars movie?"

"Yep."

" So what am I supposed to take away from this?"

"Who are you?" God asked.

"I'm Christine. A wife. A mother. A teacher."

"And?"

"Oh, and a writer?" I asked.

"Yes!" God said.

Meanwhile, in the movie, Rey said, "People keep telling me they know me. I'm afraid no one does." Geez, Rey, I can relate to you!

Luke Skywalker said, "Confronting fear is the destiny of the Jedi. Your destiny."

"I need to confront my fears as they sometimes interfere with my writing," I said.

"We've passed on all we know. A thousand generations live in you now. But this is your fight. We'll always be with you. No man's ever gone," Luke Skywalker said to Rey. And as I cried big ugly tears, my cousin, my husband and my kids stared at me in disbelief. Of course, they wouldn't understand the millions of thoughts swirling in my head at that moment. But the truth is, everything made sense. My best friend Dan's death. My grandma's. All my loved ones before. Their stories and memories are a part of me. They are all with me. They can help me write.

"The force will be with you always," Leia said.

"Christine, you have the force, the Holy Spirit. Trust it," God whispered.

"Yes, yes, yes. I get it!"

With tears in my eyes, I felt transported back to the *Lion King* movie, to Diana's cranial sacral therapy sessions, to *Frozen II* and now to Star Wars. Four different times in the past year, God in his own way asked me to know who I was and to confront any fear that I had. It's clear that we all have a purpose. And, yes, that revelation sparked my desire to write and edit like never before and ignore all the Lisas of the world who have nothing positive to say. There will always be people who are not our fans. Aristotle once said that "Knowing yourself is the beginning of all wisdom." And who would have thought that the start of my wisdom would come from my being reminded of who I am through some movies and physical therapy sessions for my neck. God can and will use any situation to get your attention.

Conclusion: Final Thoughts

The living, loving God of the universe has spoken throughout history, and still speaks today — not just to pastors or priests, but to anyone who will listen. God will speak to you. No matter what spiritual condition you find yourself in, if you train your ear to be open to heaven, God will speak.

— Bill Hybels

In looking back at the events in our lives, many of us will see how synchronicity plays a role — how we meet certain people at key times in life when we most need them. Many of these encounters are not just happenstance or coincidence. Rather, it is the purposeful lining up of events and people to help us fulfill our soul's purpose. Sometimes these encounters are not always positive, but God uses them to draw us closer to him as he did throughout my journey. In doing so, God helped me figure out my career as a teacher, led me to my husband and children, as well as inspired me to write this book. God will use whatever means possible to get our attention. People will often hear God's whispers when reading the Bible, but for others, as well as for me, it may be that intuitive thought that pops up, that feeling to reach out or call someone for no reason at all. It might be seeing how events keep aligning, which can provide confirmation that you're on the right track. That synchronicity that you thought was random, might prove to be purposeful. It might be the words in a song, book, or license plate that comes about and rings true for you. Or it could even be a prophetic dream that you write off, thinking it's nothing important.

The bottom line is that no pastor, healer, counselor, parent, spouse, or friend can tell you with one hundred percent accuracy what God's whispers are or what they mean for you. That, my friend, is up to you to figure out. And how do you figure out God's whispers? First, realize that God wants to have a relationship with you right now. He wants you to speak to him as much as he wants to speak to you. Once you realize that God is here through the Holy Spirit or whatever name you want to give it, trust that he speaks to you all the time in multiple ways. Have faith like a child and hear God's whispers, knowing it is okay if you make mistakes. When you miss God's whispers, learn from it, take a risk and step out and listen again. In Jeremiah 29:13, he says, "You will seek me and find me when you search for me with all your heart." Basically, no one ever changed the world playing it safe. Following God and the Holy Spirit is scary, but wouldn't it be even more scary not to?

As we ride the waves of life, we will inevitably encounter storms, but if we have a relationship with God, talk to and listen to him, that's the best life preserver possible. As Jesus says in Matthew 7:7, "Ask and it will be given to you; seek and you will find; knock and the door will be opened to you." As you listen to God and obey his whispers, what you seek in your heart will be fulfilled one way or another. It may not be your way, but these whispers will be a gateway of hope for you as you continue to thrive through the ebb and flow of life's horrific storms and miraculous rainbows.

While editing this book and wondering if there was anything I missed and needed to add, God came to me in a dream. God stated that I needed to explain what people should do when they feel He is silent and waiting for him to speak to provide guidance in their lives. From my stories of infertility and miscarriage, my need for answers when I couldn't hear God's voice led me on the wrong path by trusting other people instead of trusting God. So what do people do, and how do they avoid taking the wrong path when God is silent? As God asked me to add these ideas, I felt perplexed. Here, I wrote a whole book on how God speaks, but what can people do when they are thirsty for answers in the desert and can't hear a thing?

"Phil, how do I answer that question? Any ideas? I must answer it because everyone will have moments of silence with God. It's inevitable."

"I don't know, but I'm sure God will give you an answer if you keep asking him, or maybe we ask Pastor Tom for his thoughts on it."

I kid you not, readers. A minute later, God answered my question. Phil just happened to put on his audio-book, *Talking with Your Kids about God* by Natasha Crain, and the answer appeared. Not having all the answers allows us "to depend humbly on God rather than depend pridefully on ourselves." When I didn't have the answers to my different medical challenges and other life dilemmas, I needed to trust and rely on God, which made me pray and seek a relationship with him. The more I turned to God, the more I noticed his ways of communicating with me. The answer, dear readers, is that we need to trust and rely on God even in moments of silence. Doing that is not always smooth sailing, but the calm after the storm is worth the wait.

While waiting on God to speak proved challenging at times, it helped me to realize that God's silence was purposeful and for my benefit. Sometimes I just needed to be patient and trust that things would work out. God had my back! Crain stated in her book, "When we're faced with uncertain or missing answers, we can be confident that those pages were intentionally left blank." There is no way for us to understand the all-encompassing knowledge of the past, present, and future that God has. Sometimes we hope and pray for something, yet our prayers go unanswered because having that prayer fulfilled, may not be best for us. We can't always realize that, though, until we look back on our lives and see God's hand in it. Perhaps God's silence is a call for you to seek and rely on Him. And your waiting for an answer to prayer, whether it be days, weeks, or years or never, might be God's knowing what is needed in his perfect timing. In Proverbs 3:5 states, "Trust in the Lord with all your heart and lean not on your own understanding." This is what I had to learn. This is what I'm still learning. And this is what God wants you to learn too. Don't wait! He's there, waiting to listen and talk to you.

A Request from the Author

My hope is that you too will see how God speaks in multiple ways in your own life. As God guides you through your various journeys, please feel free to write me and share your own stories of faith. I would love to hear about them. Best wishes as you ride the waves of life with God as your captain and life preserver. Blessings!

You can write me at: **christineneksauthor@gmail.com**

You can check out my website at: **christinenekasthoma.com.**

You can follow me on my Facebook author page at: **https://www.facebook.com/christinenekasthoma.**

You can follow me on Instagram at: **christine.n.thoma** *or Twitter:* **@thomachristine**

Acknowledgements

First, I must thank the One whose Spirit nudged me to write down all the events that happened to me throughout the years to help give my life meaning and purpose and for showing me the ways that the Holy Spirit speaks to inspire, guide and heal. Thank you, God.

To my dear and loving husband, Phil, who believed and encouraged me to write from the beginning. He never doubted the importance of this book and the need for me to publish it. To my two boys, Beckett and Gavin, who are great lights in my life and answers to many prayers. To the birth parents — Jo Anna, Derek, Amanda, Danny and their families for trusting us to be their child's parents. We love you all very much.

To my parents, Bob and Rita Nekas for their unconditional love. They told me at a young age that I was a writer and that like *The Little Engine That Could*, that "I can" do whatever I put my mind to. To my grandparents, Amata and Emil Schiesser, who encouraged me to "keep writing"; they were the best pen pals. To my late Uncle Emil who encouraged me not to give up and who inspired me with his stories of NASA.

To my favorite high school English teacher, Mrs. Cantwell and Professor Greene who both challenged me and believed in my ability to write. To Georgia Heard who taught me how to appreciate, write, and teach poetry.

To the late Dan Tietz whose friendship inspired me to be a better person and to live each moment like it's my last. To Tori, Amy, Cheryl, Stephanie, Sara, Mollie, Megan, Nina, Jen, Jan, Erica and too many numerous other family and friends who lift me up, encourage, and inspire me. Thank you for being there through it all.

To my colleagues, students and their families — both past and present — who often listened intently to my stories commenting that I should write a book. Thank you for your interest and support.

To Nicole Bjork, Lydia Schleicher, and Jamie Lovejoy who each read a very rough version of this book when it was only half written and gave me insightful advice.

To Amy Reese, Barb Geiger, Melinda Larson, Nancy Flinchbaugh, and Kathie Giorgio who read and gave suggestions for editing; their critical and constructive feedback helped make this book what it is today.

Finally, I am grateful to Rebecca Benston and the staff at Higher Ground Books & Media for believing in me and in the merit of this story. I admire their mission.

Other titles from Higher Ground Books & Media:

Raven Transcending Fear by Terri Kozlowski

The Deception of 666 by Terra Kern

Forgiven and Not Forgotten by Terra Kern

The Power of Knowing by Jean Walters

Through the Sliver of a Frosted Window by Robin Melet

Breaking the Cycle by Willie Deeanjlo White

Journey to Jesus by Rev. Jerry C. Crossley

Despising the Shame by Talia Stone

Bits and Pieces by Rebecca Whited

Finding Purpose in the Pain by Brenda W. McIntyre

Healing in God's Power by Yvonne Green

Losing the Sound of Your Own Stride by Stephen Shepherd

Chronicles of a Spiritual Journey by Stephen Shepherd

The Real Prison Diaries by Judy Frisby

The Words of My Father by Mark Nemetz

The Bottom of This by Tramaine Hannah

Add these titles to your collection today!

http://www.highergroundbooksandmedia.com

HIGHER GROUND BOOKS & MEDIA IS
AN INDEPENDENT PUBLISHER

Do you have a story to tell?

Higher Ground Books & Media is an independent Christian-based publisher specializing in stories of triumph! Our purpose is to empower, inspire, and educate through the sharing of personal experiences. We are always looking for great, new stories to add to our collection. If you're looking for a publisher, get in touch with us today!

Please be sure to visit our website for our submission guidelines.

http://www.highergroundbooksandmedia.com/submission-guidelines

HGBM SERVICES IS OUR CONSULTING FIRM

AUTHOR SERVICES

HGBM Services offers a variety of writing and coaching services for aspiring authors! We can help with editing, manuscript critiques, self-publishing, and much more! Get in touch today to see how we can help you make your dream of becoming an author a reality!

*****

We also offer social media marketing services for authors, small businesses, and non-profit organizations. Let us help you get the word out about your book, your projects, and your mission. We offer great rates, quality promos, consistent communication, and a personal touch!

http://www.highergroundbooksandmedia.com/editing-writing-services

Need Bulk Copies?

If you would like to order bulk copies of this book or any other title at Higher Ground Books & Media, please contact us at highergroundbooksandmedia@gmail.com.

We offer discounts for purchases of 20 or more copies. Excellent for small groups, book clubs, classrooms, etc.

Get in touch today and get a set of great stories for your students or group members.

Made in the USA
Monee, IL
22 January 2023

25904758R00144